SNOWB[OARDING]

FOR
WOMEN

a guide for the Betty Shred wannabe

Text and Drawings by
Chickie Rosenberg

Show Dog Snowboard Press, LLC
Box 1069
Killington, Vermont 05751

www.SnowboardingForWomen.com

ISBN 0-9744658-0-1
Library of Congress Control Number:2003095921

Second Printing, 2003

Printed in the United States of America

Daamen, Inc. Printing Company
Industrial Park
West Rutland, Vermont 05777

Inspiration

I owe my inspiration for this endeavor to the wonderful people to whom I have given snowboarding lessons. Their overwhelmingly enthusiastic response to my coaching has provided a positive endorsement of my approach to teaching.

Dedication

I dedicate this book to my husband, Paul Rosenberg, without whose emotional support and encouragement to achieve goals beyond my own expectations, I never would have had the opportunity to devote so much of my life to this sport which I love. Paul converted me from a flatlander tennis player to a diehard snowboarding Betty Shred.

Warning–Disclaimer

This book has been written to provide information on snowboarding. It is a guide in preparing a woman in terms of how to dress, necessary accessories, selection of equipment, and what to anticipate when learning to snowboard. It is not intended to be a do-it-yourself guide nor is it at all a substitute for a professionally directed lesson. In fact, it is not even meant to be a guide book for other instructors, as different snowboard professionals follow their own procedures for teaching and have their own methods of instruction.

Snowboarding for Women: a guide for the Betty Shred wannabe was written to convince women that snowboarding can be a positive experience, despite the fears and trepidations so many have expressed in regard to the sport. The purpose of this book is to allay those fears, encourage involvement, and explain what could take place in a lesson in order to eliminate fear of the unknown. When one has some idea of what to expect, it will be easier to handle the actual experience.

The author has tried to cover subjects of importance to the beginner snowboarder; however, the information discussed herein should be interpreted as a highly individualistic and often idiosyncratic guide and not as an ultimate source for snowboarding information. Furthermore, this book contains information on snowboarding equipment and email addresses that are current only up to the printing date.

The author and publisher will not be responsible to any person or entity for any injury or damage alleged to have been caused, directly or indirectly, by any of the information or instructional procedures described in this book.

About the Author

Chickie R.

In 1990, Chickie Rosenberg began instructing snowboarding as one of the original staff of one woman and six men at Killington Ski and Snowboard Resort in Killington, VT, the largest ski and snowboard resort in eastern North America. Today, she is part of their snowboarding team of more than one hundred instructors. Over the years, Chickie has taught more people who have, in turn, become snowboard instructors than anyone else on the Killington staff. She has developed a wide reputation for coaching women and is known for giving a *no falls* lesson which has earned her a following of loyal students. At Killington, she is one of the leaders in coaching special three day clinics for women only. Her achievement of the coveted Level II certification by the American Association of Snowboard Instructors (AASI), her years of teaching, active participation in regional training clinics, and extensive riding at resorts in North America, South America, and Europe have given her a broad perspective on the joy that women can achieve through snowboarding.

Chickie is a frequent contributor to *Snow Pro*, the official publication of the Professional Ski Instructors of America-Eastern Education Foundation (PSIA/AASI). She also wrote a series of articles for *Fresh and Tasty,* a snowboarding magazine for women. Chickie is the editor of

Show Dog, Killington's in-house publication which goes to a teaching staff of over 500 instructors.

Just in case you may think of a snowboard instructor as lacking in diverse cultural interests, Chickie is a docent at The Newark Museum in Newark, N.J., where, along with giving art tours to the public, as an expert in African art she has written on the museum's collection, *Art of Africa: The Newark Museum Knowledge Cards,* recently published by Pomegranate Communications, Inc., Catalog Number K151, Box 6099 Rohnert Park, CA 94927, www.pomegranate.com.

An undergraduate degree in English at Muhlenberg College and an M.A. from New York University are academic credentials, and years of teaching on the high school and college level plus communication skills applied in free lance writing are but one part of the picture of an energetic and enthusiastic coach. But the true essence of her talent which has made her outstanding in her field is the fact that Chickie has a deep love for snowboarding and a sincere belief that it is particularly suited to the feminine sensibility. In this book she has set out the guidelines, explained the process, offered advice on taking lessons, and written a very detailed account of everything to expect from what to wear on the slopes to what to cook for dinner that night back at the condo.

So, what are you waiting for? Get started reading and be ready to fall in love with a sport you never dreamed of participating in, and look forward to your newfound self-identity as a **Betty Shred!**

CONTENTS

Why
Snowboard?

INTRODUCTION

Here is the situation: your friends are all excited about snowsports, and you would like to join them for a weekend get-away in the mountains; or, your boyfriend, husband, or significant other is eager for you to take up the sport which certainly adds a lot of pressure. Yes, snowboarding may be the fastest growing winter sport in America, but is it really the right activity for you? You hate the cold, you are afraid of heights, and you don't like the idea of going fast downhill. Family or business responsibilities would make physical injury a severe hardship. On top of that, one hears that when learning to snowboard you spend the entire time falling which certainly doesn't sound like a lot of fun. Whether you have someone to travel with or not, as a beginner you would be alone in that you have no one to join with you when signing up for lessons. So, why snowboard?

I am always amazed at the fact that I am a snowboard instructor. I had never liked cold weather, mostly because it seemed as if I could never get warm enough. Although I fortunately do not suffer from any diagnosed medical condition, nevertheless, my feet and hands are usually ice cold. I was certainly not a good candidate for a cold weather sport, much less, one which would be labeled as "extreme."

My husband was a skier and had tried to get me to accompany him on the slopes, but I definitely was not at all interested in doing so. Forever hopeful, on our honeymoon he had even secretly stowed away his ski boots in a corner of the car trunk, just in case a ski opportunity might arise. How did he entice me from favoring tennis, an activity which is done on a ground level surface which is flat, in the sunshine, wearing comfortable sneakers and those fashionable little outfits? Those last words were the key. He decided to take me shopping to select the latest style in skiwear. The next obvious step would be that I would want to wear them. It worked...,but even though I actually came to enjoy skiing, I was still unhappy about always being cold.

There were two breakthroughs for me. The first was taking an advanced skier's week program at Killington during an unusually bitter cold spell. My instructor, Janet Shimp, advised her Mountain Group participants to dress for the cold "in layers." I had always thought that long underwear, sweater, and outerwear jacket would suffice. She revealed that she had on clothing layered upon layer, to the point where she needed oversized warm-up pants (Note that this was some 15 years ago, well before the existence of today's high tech non bulky materials for skiwear). I went shopping again but this time purchased jacket and pants sized slightly larger than the ones I already had and learned to fill up all that roominess with layers of clothing. It worked! Truly, the reason I have overcome hesitancy to do snow sports is because I have learned how to dress. Chapter 2 discusses the principles involved, but, in essence, I simply accept the fact that I, even today, must wear a layer or two more of clothing than someone else. This is true to the extent that in our staff locker room, my fellow ski and snowboard pros ask how many layers I am putting on, and then they laughingly guide themselves with at least one layer less! I know what I need to stay warm. Your own awareness of personal requirements in the amount of layering for body warmth will change your definition of "dress for success." Being comfortable in the cold enabled me to become an enthusiastic skier.

My second breakthrough was in learning to snowboard. Why try snowboarding? For people who are sensitive to the cold, snowboarding is truly the sport of choice. Learning to snowboard is very physical in that you will be down on the snow, rolling around and generally doing a lot of physical body movement so that even when you have advanced to higher elevations (and more wind chill), you will still find that the body motions necessary in riding a snowboard actually help to keep you warm. Also, when I took up snowboarding I never had to resort to purchasing oversized clothing; the baggy style of snowboardwear allows for a multitude of layers, perfect for an over bundled person like me, and the new materials keep one warm without making you look like an oversized puff ball. An added bonus is that the snowboarder learning area is usually on the lower mountain where it is warmer (and closer to the lodge).

By the way, if you are hesitant because your friends are all advanced skiers or snowboarders who would not be with you (or even if you have no one to go with to the resort), that is rather an advantage in some ways. Sign up for a group introductory lesson. This offers a sense of privacy in that your friends will therefore not be witnesses to your learning situation. One loses self consciousness when learning in a group of strangers who are all in the same situation of being newcomers to the sport. Another plus of the group lesson is that people tend to bond. Although the actual time spent together in the lesson may be brief, friendships are forged, resulting in your having met people on your own ability level.

Snowboarding for Women

Group members tend to stay together after class is over which means that you will now have company with whom you can practice riding. An extra bonus will be the fact that because you all learned together, you will have in common a shared knowledge and understanding of standard snowboarding basics.

Fear of heights is not really an easy matter to overcome. I find it akin to the fact that I fly in airplanes. I don't enjoy flying, but, nevertheless, I still do so   rather than face alternative modes of transportation. The same is true for the chairlift. Ground level lifts are called "drags" in Europe and I think that is a fitting description as these ground surface lift methods of propulsion are simply to drag a person uphill. The most frightened I have ever been on a lift was in Chile when taking a seemingly never ending t-bar. The rope tows, pomas and t-bars in the States are not quite so harrowing, although in comparison, the chair lift starts to look very appealing. Among the advantages of the chair lift is that it moves quickly, one is usually not alone so there is companionship to help relieve personal stress, and **I never look down!** Yes, I have been instructing   for ever so many years and   have skied and snowboarded all over the world, but I never ever look down from a chairlift. The best way to defeat vertigo is simply not to allow it to happen.

There is a Vermont state law which requires that chair lift riders must have the safety bar down and in place. In the western resorts...that's another story. Just focus on all those tiny five and six year olds happily riding on the chair ahead of you. Usually, by the time you will get to taking a chairlift, you will be stoked on snowboarding anyway, so fear of heights will not be effective as a deterrent. Another comforting fact is that most of the larger ski areas have trams or cable cars to whisk

iv

you up the mountain. The same rule applies there as for the chair lift: look out, look up, but don't look down!

Injury is always a possibility, but if you are cautious and if you take a lesson with a professional instructor, you should be safe. Whenever I question persons about an accident, it is usually due to being on terrain which was above their skill level, or they were fooling around, or they had a friend coaching them. Knowing how to ride does not mean knowing how to teach someone to ride. Unfortunately, the most commonly stated words of encouragement one hears on the mountain is, "Don't worry. You can do it." This is said by the so-called friend who has placed his companion in a situation having overestimated that person's ability to handle it. What is easy to do for an experienced snowboarder is far from easy for the novice. Even if the skill level is there, FEAR takes over in capital letters, and the scene is set for injury. Don't let this happen to you. Take a group or private lesson with a snowboarding professional.

While on the subject of fear, this is an always present factor for many people. In fact, there are those women who decide to do snowboarding, an extreme sport, just to face and conquer their fears. The best counter to fear is confidence, and the best way to build confidence is by convincing yourself that you have attained the necessary skill level for the terrain you have selected. Since we tend to be our own most severe judge, confidence usually comes slowly. Practice the moves and take repeated lessons because a clinic from last season or even last month becomes vague in your memory, and you may be wasting the opportunity to improve by practicing what are poorly remembered or improper movements.

In case you have already "tried" it, that doesn't really

mean you have mastered snowboarding. An unfortunate situation is that in marketing the sport, ski areas tend to advertise a learn to snowboard lesson with the implication that this initial clinic will be the total instruction you will ever have to take. Learning to snowboard simply means learning some of the basics. There's a lot more to it all than could ever be taught in several hours and than could ever be absorbed in such a short time. I often wonder about people who proudly state that they have had one lesson and then gone on a black diamond (expert) trail. Do they think that having done so means they are experts? I interpret it that they are rather stupid and were lucky to have come down unscathed! But such comments tend to be a "guy thing"; women are usually, by nature, more responsible in terms of personal risk.

I happen to think that snowboarding is a sport which is particularly appealing to women in terms of the fact that the balance movements involved in riding are so much like dancing. In fact, many of my better students have been involved in dance whether ballet or ballroom. Rhythm, balance, and precision of body movement are all part of the snowboard choreography. A skier once commented to me that as he skied behind me it looked as if I was floating down the trail. It looked so effortless. That is part of the lure of snowboard riding.

Again, if I could snowboard, then you can do it. I am not a big strong athletic person, and I started to snowboard at the absurdly advanced age of 50! It all seemed so crazy, but it was so much fun that I decided not to rationalize about it but just to do it. I had determination and confidence that I would persevere until mastery. Those are the necessary ingredients: stubbornness and a determination to succeed. There are no wimps who snowboard. It is not a simple process to snowboard, so those who are afraid to try hard and those who like a quick learn do not last very long in a clinic lesson. On the other hand, the gal who insists that she will meet the challenge will certainly finish up as an accomplished Betty Shred !!!

1
Answers/Questions

Around 1990 during a time when logo t-shirts were the height of fashion, *Transworld Snowboarding* magazine sold an "answer" shirt which had the following message emblazoned on its back:

Top Five Answers
1. **It's called a snowboard.**
2. **Yes, it's fun.**
3. **No, it's actually quite easy.**
4. **Yes, I can stop it and even turn!**
5. **No, I don't ski anymore.**

If those were the answers, then what were the questions?

Answer #1: It's called a snowboard.
Question #1: What is it?

Back then, answer number one was not so very obvious. It was not unusual for snowboarders to be one of a very select few to appear at mountain resorts. In fact, the very rarity of meeting a fellow snowboarder contributed to an overall spirit of comradery. Method of snowsport transportation became a means of entry to friendship with snowboarders greeting each other and taking runs together, simply for the novelty of riding with a fellow boarder. Age and sex were not factors; many times I spent an afternoon riding on the mountain as a response to an invitation for companionship with someone well less than half my age. Regarding the equipment, even today people seem to mistakenly refer to the snowboard as a skiboard.

Answer #2: Yes, it's fun.
Question #2: Is it fun?

Although I am obviously wearing my resort instructor's uniform, people constantly ask me if I like to snowboard. Would I be doing it if I didn't like it? My answer to the preference over skiing is that snowboarding is simply much more fun. That's what snowboarding is all about: the enjoyment of a sport which gives you a sense of liberation and escape. It's a social activity which you can enjoy with your friends. It brings you outdoors, provides a personal challenge, and gives, in return for the effort, a feeling of excitement and a refreshing break with the everyday routine. Snowboarding releases a sense of freedom which is totally exhilarating.

Answer #3: No, it's actually quite easy.
Question #3: Is it hard to do?

Another question I am always asked is regarding the process of learning. My response is to advise that people should take a lesson. There is nothing like instruction with a qualified professional. These instructors differ from your snowboarding friends in that they have been specifically trained to teach the various learning skills. The purpose of this book is to provide background understanding which is a supplement to, not substitute for, the professionally administered lesson. The more you know about snowboarding, whether how to dress, what equipment to select, or even how to create a turn, the easier it will be to get the most out of that lesson. Yes, initially snowboarding is relatively hard to learn, but once you have the basics down, it is easy to get really good at it. That is what is meant by the fast paced learning curve of snowboarding.   Graphed, it would look somewhat like a reversed capital C with the initial line running horizontal, but then the slope increases and the line goes up and up and up as you quickly get better and better and better.

Answer #4: Yes, I can stop it and even turn!
Question #4: Can you control the board ?

With snowboarding's above mentioned well known learning curve, one certainly attains a level of accomplishment faster in snowboarding than with so many other snowsports. It just requires patience and perseverance during that first day. You will quickly learn to stop and even turn, thus controlling your destiny while slipping and sliding.

Answer #5: No, I don't ski anymore. Question #5: Do you prefer snowboarding to skiing?

This last answer is probably the most revealing one. I, personally, have not skied in over 13 years. If anyone had ever told me that there would be a winter sport which would replace my joy of skiing, I would never have believed it. I had advanced to the level of being a ski instructor, yet once I had learned how to snowboard, each time I saw a boarder on the mountain when I was on alpine equipment, I felt a tinge of envy. I requested a transfer to teaching snowboarding and never looked back!

The *Transworld Snowboarding* shirt pretty much said it all, except that I would have added one additional answer:

Answer #6: Yes, and they are usually even better than the men!
You can figure out what the question would have been.

Oh my!
I haven't a
thing
to wear!

2
You Can't Have Fun if You're Cold
A Guide for Clothing
(and Miscellaneous Accessories)

Most books on snowboarding begin with a presentation in terms of a history of the sport followed by an analysis of equipment, all as an introduction before the instructional material. At this point, snowboarding history isn't really of much interest to you; furthermore, you must have already decided to take up snowboarding or you wouldn't have chosen to read this book. Because we all well know the adage that looking good is most of the game, let us instead begin with with the more relevant subject of what the properly dressed snowboarding woman should wear. After all, you can rent the board and boots at the mountain, but what you wear must be carefully thought out and obtained in advance.

In the sport of snowboarding, although people may appear casually dressed without the sleek matched outfits of a skier, such impromptu looks may be deceptive. Actually, their clothing has usually been specifically selected. When the ski bunny gets cold or tired , she retires to the lodge and sits by the fire. When beginner Betty Shred quits, she is often not just

25

cold and tired, but, in addition, could find herself soaking wet. One cannot expect to learn a new sport when chilled and wet which will be the case if you are not properly dressed. Also, don't kid yourself; when you look good, you do well. Wearing the right clothes will give you physical comfort, a more positive outlook, plus a determination to succeed given the monetary investment in your new duds. You're going to love snowboarding, everybody does, and you'll love it even more if you are warm, dry, and look great! Anyway, since when do women really have to be convinced to go shopping? Follow these guidelines for clothing selection, and you will not only last out the lesson dry, warm, and in comfort but also enjoy it more.

You surely are aware that snowboarders in their loose baggy clothes have a different style of dress from skiers. This is because, particularly when learning, you will be very actively using your entire body and, as a result, even on a cold day, often working up a sweat. In fact, when I teach a beginner group we sometimes have to make a clothing pile on the side of the trail as people become so overheated that it is necessary to strip off some of those unnecessary layers. On the other hand, the opposite clothing problem may arise in clinic groups when chattering teeth indicate that there has not been the best choice made in clothing selection. Whether being damp with sweat from being overheated or chilled because you are not warm enough, there is a way to dress which prepares you in either case. This chapter will deal with how the body actually processes temperature adjustments along with suggestions for appropriate clothing product selections.

Since most of the snowboard season is when temperatures are low, one must dress accordingly. I teach in

Chapter 2 You Can't Have Fun if You're Cold

Vermont which is known for its cold winters, but winter is winter. Just because you are going out West does not mean it will always be warm. Don't be thrown off by the magazine ads which picture women in bright sunshine wearing those cute little headbands. If it's cold enough to maintain snow, then it's usually fairly cold (except for spring conditions which usually occur in late March or April).

The various factors to be considered are temperature, wind chill, amount of sunshine, time of day, and where you plan to be on the mountain. A comfort is that your travel friends may be experienced riders and therefore will be out there high on the upper trails, but as a beginning snowboarder you will find yourself on lower more shallow terrain where it is usually more sheltered from the elements, not as cold, and, ultimately closer to the lodge where you can duck in to warm up.

Basic Premise

There are two aspects of dressing for the cold which are often not known to the novice and have particular relevance to women. The first involves headgear. Women do not like to wear hats. Period. We all know this because wearing a hat messes up your hair and leaves you with that awful "hat-head" look. The easiest way to explain the importance of wearing a hat is that you should think of your body as a house and your head is the chimney. If your head is uncovered, all the heat will rise straight up out of your body! It is as simple as that. If you are cold, put on a hat; if you wish to be warm, wear a hat. Note that "hat" does not mean "headband" which only protects your ears and does not prevent body heat loss. While on the subject, a better choice than a hat is that of a helmet. If helmets are worn for biking, and motorcycling, and in-line skating, then why not for snowboarding? The advantages of the helmet are many (see Chapter 3). Aside from the safety factor, they really keep you incredibly warm even on the coldest days. Also, there is the added bonus that they are totally fashionable in terms of snowboarding. They make you look as if you know what you are doing out there.

"But," you say, "it's not my head that gets cold. It's my hands and feet." Not what you think! First of all, snowboard boots are warm. But the more pertinent answer to this problem of extremities involves the second aspect of winter dressing. The savvy snowsport person knows that hands and feet get cold because the body's circulatory system has gone into emergency mode. Because your heat is presumably going out of that open chimney of the no-hat-head, the kidneys have sent out an alert signal. The circulatory system draws the blood from the extremities to help warm the body trunk, leaving fingers and toes numb with cold. Put on a warm hat or helmet, grab an extra layer for your upper body, and your toes will stay warm.

The other aspect to be considered is the fact that snowboarding involves a physical workout. As stated earlier, even on a cold day, you will perspire. If you are wearing the wrong kind of undergarments, that sweat will stay as a layer of moisture soaking your clothing, leaving you cold and uncomfortable. You could be wearing a really warm jacket but no matter how the manufacturer has convinced you of the quality of this outerwear product, you must still take further precautions to be amply warm. Those are the theories of dressing. Now for some specifics.

On Layering

I mentioned in the introduction how a lesson with one of our Killington ski pros taught me how to dress for the mountain. It was one of those bitter cold sub-zero days in Vermont. I was shivering, and my ski instructor asked me if I had layered my clothing. I was wearing a very heavy wool sweater and had wrongly thought that would suffice. The fine art of layering is based upon the theory that body heat is sandwiched and insulated between the various layers of clothing creating little pockets of warm air. Because of today's high technology fabrics, the layering need not be cumbersome; thin fabrics, if they are the right kind, do the job without bulking you up. Anyway, as a snowboarder there is no problem fitting multiple layers underneath because of our baggy style of outerwear.

Underwear: First Layer

The first purchase you must make is for a set of long underwear made of any of those new fabrics which, as their advertising states, "wick away body moisture." Years ago one may have worn wool which is not only itchy but also stays damp. Cotton absorbs and holds the moisture, another poor choice. Silk is advertised as retaining warmth, but remember how silk blouses tend to show underarm perspiration stains? That's because the fabric doesn't breathe; again, a poor choice. To insure the fact that you are not going to be cold from body moisture soaked undergarments, look for items made from moisture wicking fabric, which usually go under designations of "polypropylene" tagged with vocabulary such as "moisture permeable," "bi-ply," "wicking," *etc.*   The various manufacturers seem to have their own names for their individually registered trademarked materials. DuPont's "Cool-Max," Patagonia's "Capilene," Burton's "DryRide," Medalist's "comFortel," Hot Chillys' "MicroFiber One," DuPont's "DuoFold Vent-A-Layer" made of "ThermaStat" are just a few of the many choices. Do not be prejudiced by your natural fibers preference instinct. These are really great products with unique hydrophobic (water rejecting) abilities. Their technology allows channel fibers to move moisture away from the skin and therefore will keep you comfortably dry.

You should wear a first layer, top and bottom, made of one of those high tech fabrics. I personally like the product line Hot Chillys which are of this type of fabric blend , and because the bottoms are tights (get the ones without stirrups as you will not want that extra material in your boot), there is no bulk so that you can easily wear a second layer over them, if needed, of fleece leggings for those bitter super cold days. What's in <u>my</u> snowboarding underwear dresser drawer? The abovementioned Hot Chillys tights, men's Polarmax performance thermal wear tops (for some reason, the men's line of this company's products seem to be warmer than their women's products), Patagonia Capilene tops, Hot Chillys fleece leggings, and Hot Chillys fleece zip neck tops.

There are so many new and high quality products out there. Check out items from Patagonia Company (they offer 6 different weights of layering underwear), Burton, L.L. Bean, Eddie Bauer, and of course, don't overlook your local ski/snowboarding shop's inventory. In fact, the latter mentioned ski shops along with Patagonia and Burton will have the best choices since they are entirely focused on outdoor sport clothing, whereas L.L. Bean and Eddie Bauer are more diverse in their offerings and can't really compare in terms of depth of snowboard-specific selection. Read those labels and select wisely. For those who like to do virtual shopping, be sure to check out the listings at the end of this chapter.

Turtleneck Shirt

After that first layer of polypropylene, I then wear one of those high tech material or cotton blend turtleneck shirts. If it is really cold out, I usually prefer to wear fleece. This keeps the neck area warm. For those who hate tight neckwear, there are companies who make zipper necks.

Sweater

Next would come a sweater, either wool or fleece. Historically, ski sweaters were those bulky knits which were heavy weight so one presumed that they were exceedingly warm; but, think again. Actually, the really warmest sweater with the added bonus of no bulk is cashmere. In case you are put off by the high price of such a quality item, try checking out the sale racks of your favorite department (non-ski/snowboard) store. You would be amazed at the number of reduced for clearance cashmere sweaters out there, especially at the end of the season. Size is not too crucial, as the bigger the better to use for layering over that turtleneck and long underwear top. Color is not so important as it may not show (possibly sandwiched under a second sweater), and anyway, snowboarders are truly not inhibited by fashion color coordinates. Thin wool sweaters are also good. Remember, it's the layering which creates and holds the warmth, not the heavy weight of the knit.

Some companies, such as Ibex (www.ibexwear.com) have even improved upon wool, using technology to improve insulation from dampness and wind. Smartwool (www.smartwool.com) uses Merino wool which is constructed to keep you warm, not damp, and not bulky. Stay far away from cotton, as it does not provide warmth, and worse, it holds in moisture from perspiration. Beware...I have seen many ski theme design sweaters on the market which are made of cotton. It is imperative to read the fabric content labels.

Fleece vests are handy to have as they warm the central body organs without bulk around the arms. Or instead, a fleece pullover shirt goes perfectly on top of that thin sweater or in place of it. Fleece has an added advantage in that it is machine washable and is not vulnerable to hungry summer moths during the off season.

Variation in Dress for Extreme Cold: Brrrrr

Actually, it is only really bitter cold in midwinter. This is true out West along with the Northeast regions. The coldest temperature I have ever experienced on a ski trip was in Steamboat, Colorado, early in February. In fact, it was so cold that the mountain had been closed the previous week. Therefore, for January or February, it is usually necessary to consider supplementing the layering process I have mentioned when dressing for near zero temperatures with the additional influencing factors of wind chill and lack of sunshine. On the bottoms, over the moisture wicking first layer comes a second of fleece. In extreme cases I have even resorted to a mid weight underwear bottom layer sandwiched between the Hot Chillys and the fleece. Remember that although you may have a warmer jacket to protect your upper body, usually one's wardrobe is limited to a single pair of snowboard pants, whatever the weight. Upper body warmth is easier. Just pile on the various layers, with fleece as the best fabric choice.

Jacket

Thirty years ago the only waterproof breathable fabric on the market was the new (and expensive) invention of Gore-Tex. Today there are so very many fabrics out there that it's virtually impossible to list them all properly. The main thing to keep in mind is that when reading the labels check to see words such as "breathable" and know the direction of your concern which is to move water vapor (produced by body perspiration) outward. This is *breathability* as opposed to *waterproofing* which prevents water from coming inward. Remember, unless you plan to spend a lot of time out there on rainy days, it is basically the seat of a snowboarder's pants where waterproofing is necessary and most appreciated.

Choose your jacket carefully, as snowboarding jackets differ from those of skiers. Their design is more functional in that this sport involves upper body movement which means that loose fitting cuts and venting offer comfort while the longer length allows one to bend over to make binding adjustments without having the jacket hike up to your waist. Lots of pockets are always a bonus.

In case you may wonder why I have devoted so much attention to the first and middle clothing layers, and so little to this third outermost layer, it is because today's snowboard specific jackets are so well designed to meet the demands of the sport that you don't need a lot of guidance here. Gone are those puffy unisex ski jackets which left you looking like a tire advertising mannequin. The shops now have a variety of high profile designs for women with a multitude of features. Try them on, and ask the sales help for snowboard specific guidance.

Burton's equipment for women catalog offers a full analysis of its various product choices with labeling defined with a vocabulary of "access," "tri-lite," "tactic,""toast," "bio-lite," *etc.* One of the new fabrics used by Burton is "Gore Airvantage" which actually uses air as an insulation element. Another product making its premiere for the 2004 season line are Burton jackets insulated with Aerogels Spaceloft, the insulation used in the NASA space shuttle. Bonfire's jackets are of "Vaporite" fabric which is described as having "twintec" microporous coating; NorthFace uses a "Hyvent" material; Spyder has "Spyton DWR"; Columbia has "MTR, Maximum Therman Retention." The Oxford English Dictionary must have received a lot of additional submissions with all this new vocabulary! Remember to check breathability. Plastic is totally waterproof, but it certainly wouldn't be a good idea for a snowboard jacket! Hence, waterproof is not the prime desirable factor. These new fabrics offer weather protection, warmth in trapping body heat, and breathability so that body moisture is not trapped inside. Some products are now even advertising outerwear which absorbs the warmth of the sun and conversely releases excessive body heat out.

The technology is charging ahead so very fast, in fact, that there recently appeared an article in *The Wall Street Journal* on the development of a water-resistant outdoor jacket equipped with a built-in player for music downloaded from the Internet, a cell phone, headset, and a remote control. We are growing accustomed to seeing skiers and snowboarders on cell phones, and many favor the use of walkie-talkie transceivers, but the era of wearable electronics is soon to be upon us. There will be shirts with speakers and solar panels on outerwear for body warmth along with solar rechargeable jackets to act as batteries for all that built in equipment. For women, the newspaper article mentioned "an electronic sports bra that could monitor an athlete's heart rate". According to the head of Philips Interactive division at the company's Redhill research center in Britain: "Women wear bras anyway. They may as well get some extra use out of them." An interesting thought....

Pants

Skiers can stand still because they have poles to stabilize them. The snowboarder, when stopped , unless the surface is really flat, will be more comfortable when sitting down. The problem is that sitting means that you are on a surface of wet snow and often for extended periods of time. Therefore, it is really important to wear the right kind of outerwear pants. Forget about jeans. They are actually like blotters, attracting and absorbing water. Water resistant pants are simply a MUST. Look at the design of many snowboard pants, and you will see that they often have inserted a heavy (waterproof) section on the seat offering added protection from the snow. Another thing to look for when purchasing snowboard pants are built in pockets inside at the knee for (foam) pads. Not absolutely necessary, but a nice feature. When not sitting in the snow, one is kneeling on the snow. Knees get cold, wet, and sometimes battered. External knee pads are fine, but inside pads are more subtle and comfortable, definitely a bonus. Remember when in the store trying on pants that when snowboarding you would have on at least one layer of long underwear underneath, so be sure that the waistline is ample.

Socks

For your feet, there are simple do's and do not's. **Do not** wear multiple socks. This will only restrict your blood circulation. In most cases a rental arrangement will result in your being outfitted with "soft" snowboard boots (not the hard style which looks like a ski boot). These are well insulated and will definitely keep your feet nice and warm.

Do not wear nylon stockings. They are slippery and will cause your foot to slide around in the boot. **Do** wear a good cushioned athletic sock.

Neck Gaiter

Another element of clothing which will certainly make your day outside more pleasant is the neck gaiter. This is simply an oversize fleece turtleneck which is sold with a full variety of colors in any ski shop. Lightweight and not bulky, you can easily stash it away onto the shoulder area of your jacket sleeve and whip it out for use later if you are cold. This will keep your neck and lower face warm and covered, with the added bonus of offering protection to your skin. Long scarves may look dashing but are really not a good idea as one runs the risk of becoming entangled when riding on a lift. Face masks? I thought this was about looking good.

Gloves and mittens.

No matter what the advertisers say about the waterproof quality of their gloves and mittens, they always seem to soak through rather quickly when used for snowboarding. My advice is to bring two pairs and plan to change at lunchtime. Those specifically designed for snowboarding sometimes are more water resistant than the ski variety, and Grandma's hand knits just don't make it at all. Mittens keep fingers warmer than gloves as they allow more individual finger movement, but the downside is that it is harder to negotiate bindings when wearing mittens compared to gloves. One way to keep fingers toasty warm, whether with gloves or mittens, is to purchase those little heat packs (sold at ski shops). Simply shake to activate, then set them inside. You will feel as if you've ignited a miniature furnace which provides heat throughout the day. According to Grabber My Coal Hand Warmers (telephone 800-423-1233), you "get exothermic" (whatever that means). Glove liners also work well, adding an insulating layer. An advantage of the latter is that if you must remove a mitten to make a binding adjustment, your hand is protected from the cold by the glove liner which is usually of silk or polyester knit.

Goggles and Sunglasses.

Proper eye protection is a high priority item when outdoors in the mountain environment. One tends to think of eye covering in regard to filtering the rays of the sun, but here the situation is more complex. Not only is the sun stronger in high altitudes where there is less oxygen, but there is the additional element of glaring sunlight reflected off of the snow surface. Dermatologist have made us well aware of the fact that even on cloudy days, the rays of the sun filter through. While snowboarding there is the added problem of wind and snow getting in your eyes. Skiers and snowboarders wear goggles because they are physically larger than sunglasses and therefore play an additional protective role in helping cover facial skin area otherwise exposed to the elements. One should wear goggles in the winter season when there is less sun and the days are shorter. The preferred color lens for that time of the year would be amber or pink, either of which work well in flat light situations. Add a neck gaiter and face cream, and you will be ready for those cold gusts of wind which tend to arrive late in the day when the sun goes under cloud cover. The bright sunlight of spring comes with warmer temperatures, so one should then opt for sunglasses. Preferable are the wrap around shaped frames which act as a wind screen for the side areas of the eye, particularly suitable for contact lens wearers. There are some lenses out on the market which change degree of darkness in accordance with the brightness of the sunlight, so that adds still another choice.

Miscellaneous Accessories

Face Cream

Women of all ages are concerned with their skin, and snowboarding women in particular must be aware of exposure to the damaging factors (in addition to the sensitivity to sunburn as described above) of cold, sleet and snow, windburn, and chance of frostbite. There are special creams sold at ski areas which will offer protection from the elements. It is sort of a joke among skiers in Vermont that locals know to use Bag Balm to protect their skin from excessive cold. This is an antiseptic ointment much like a very heavy Vaseline and is used by farmers to coat the teats of milk cows, protecting this tender area. Although one can sometimes find small containers in the local Vermont convenience store, it is usually sold in giant size tins, enough to last you throughout your snowboarding career. They do not seem to have a Web site, but you can write to the Dairy Association Company, Inc., Lydonville, Vermont 05851. I recently noticed that my local CVS drug store was carrying the product.

A disadvantage of Bag Balm is its lack of protection from the sun. In fact, it seems to induce sunburn. Instead, for sunny days one should consider any of the regular sun screen products you would use summertime at the beach, or check out the various creams sold at ski shops such as the products from Dermatone. This company's line features a sun screen lotion offering total protection from the sun with a zinc SPF of 36; a stick protector of SPF 23 for sun, wind and cold; a lip balm; and this instructor's steady companion: the handy "mini tin" which offers multiple protection from frostbite, wind, and also the sun. As already stated, the sun poses a serious problem with its direct rays plus snow reflection. At the western resorts there is the additional problem of high altitude sunburn. Be really careful. You learn that warm weather riding presents extra precautions because when not wearing a hat your ears and even the area where your hair parts may become severely sunburned. Even though you are packing for a winter trip, it's a good idea to remember to search for your summer beachbag and find that container of sunscreen.

Ditty Bag

A woman is never without her pocketbook...that is, unless she is snowboarding. Ski lodges have basket checks or lockers (bring plenty of quarters) where you can stash those extra items such as spare mittens, sweaters and fleece vests. Skiers have an advantage in the wearing of fanny packs, those zip pouches worn about the waist. The problem with such an accessory for the snowboarder is that in case of a fall, you will receive an impression onto your spinal cord of each stowed item, and it can prove quite painful. Backpacks look somewhat absurd. You are going snowboarding, not hiking. I actually insist that my clinic participants not wear backpacks as the weight throws off a person's natural body posture. It is hard enough for a beginner to balance on a snowboard. Adding an unnatural body weight makes it virtually impossible. The best solution is (1) take only necessities which fit into your pockets or (2) while in a ski/snowboard shop ask the clerk about a "ditty pack" which is basically a wallet worn on a cord which hangs from your neck. There is enough room for lipstick, change, and credit card, *etc.* and you won't risk having things falling out of a tightly stuffed pocket.

Lock

One last item. It's a good idea to have a ski/ snowboard lock, whether purchased or borrowed from a ski friend. Not every ski area has a snowboard check facility where, for a slight fee, you can leave your board (you are not allowed to bring snowboards into the lodge). Although you will be renting your snowboard, you are still responsible for it, and they do get stolen.

Hydration Pack

This is a relatively new accessory which is appearing

for mountain use, particularly out West or during spring season in the East, in either case when dehydration is a serious problem. Sold at ski, snowboard, and also bike shops, products are available from companies such as Safe Water whose Web site is www.safewateranywhere.com, or Platypus at www.cascadedesigns.com, Ultimate Direction www.ultimatedirection.com, Camelbak www.camelbak.com, or try the compact Micro-Stash from Backcountry Access, www.bcaccess.com. All of these companies have created water carriers which allow snowboarders to easily hydrate while riding.   The advertisement for Camelbak has a heavy duty warning which you should heed: "Hydrate or die!"

Jewelry

One last admonition-- to leave your earrings in your jewelry box. If you have ever tried pouring hot liquid into a tin container (*ie.* soup can) which you are holding, you are well aware that metal conducts heat. You need not take advanced science laboratory courses to know that the same transfer occurs with cold temperatures. Your earrings will transfer the degree of cold to the skin of your earlobes and thereby increase the danger of frostbite. On the other hand, since you are wisely wearing a warm hat or the now trendy helmet, you need not worry.   But I do keep close watch on my body-pierced snowboarding students who have rings in noses or eyebrows or other such weather exposed skin. Be a good snowboarding buddy, and act as a mirror for your friends in keeping a lookout for incipient frostbite in these areas. See Chapter 8 for details on frostbite, how to identify it, and what to do for it.

Communication Devices

The use of "talkabouts" is now ubiquitous at most ski areas. These are those hand held radios which people use on the mountain to converse with their friends and are a handy tool in order to find each other. Because the many channels are usually kept quite busy, conversations are mostly limited to discussions of which lodge, lift, or trail the separate parties are at and where they can meet. Cell phones may be the better choice in that they can also be used for emergency situations. Rather than calling 911, one can dial the mountain resort and request ski patrol help. The only problem with both of these communication devices aside from reception difficulties is that first, you will need sufficient pocket room for storage, and secondly, you will have to take off your warm gloves to hit those tiny keys. Also, having a telephone with you means that you really haven't escaped from your cares. Who wants to be receiving telephone calls when you're out there having fun?

Hopefully, this rather exhaustive discussion has neither intimidated nor discouraged you. It is simply much easier to know in advance what you will need, rather than go to the mountain and find out the hard way that you are inadequately dressed or supplied. Most towns have ski/snowboard shops which have good selections, and with the Internet one has extensive shopping options. There's always the opportunity to pick up needed equipment at a ski area where one usually has the best possible selection of items (a ready excuse for those who love to go shopping). And you can always borrow, which reminds me: **A Household Hint**. If you have opted to resurrect a jacket or pants from your past skiing history or have borrowed such clothing, you can do the following to freshen the quality of its water repellence. Wash using powder not liquid detergent. After drying, apply a water repelling spray such as Scotch-Gard.

What to Wear Summary

The forecast is for partly sunny weather, windy, high in the mid-twenties. You are in your bedroom, in bra and panties. Add the following:

on top:
> polypropylene undershirt
> Polypropylene or cotton blend turtleneck shirt
> sweater or fleece
> take along a fleece vest (just in case)
> outerwear jacket

on bottom:
> polypropylene blend tights
> (fleece leggings, optional for those who are sensitive to the cold or in case your outerwear pants are lightweight)
> socks
> snowboard pants

other items to bring along:
> 2 pairs mittens
> neck gaiter
> hat or helmet

face cream, sun protection cream
goggles, sunglasses
ski lock
ditty bag

After a day on the slopes

This is the famous *apres ski* time when all gather to discuss the day's successes or misadventures. Clothing suggestions? Blue jeans seem to be the universal choice. Wool slacks are warmer; skirts are not usually seen. Once the sun goes down, temperatures drop. This is the situation where I find that silk long underwear to be perfect as an added layer under those cotton jeans. They add a layer of warmth and do not take up any appreciable space. Since there are no sidewalks and everything is snow covered, be sure that you have packed snow boots or sturdy waterproof shoes. Leave the sneakers at home as they are wicked slippery on wet surfaces.

Spring Conditions

All of the above is fine for New England resorts and winter months, but March and April bring milder weather, particularly in the Rockies. European winters (and South America during our summers) are also warmer. I have memories of skiing wearing a bathing suit top while skiing in the afternoon and needing a down parka at night in April at Jackson Hole, Wyoming. The main thing to remember when packing for those climes is the danger of high altitude sunburn along with dehydration during the day, and the fact that, no matter what the season, it gets cold at night in the mountains.

The rules for dressing are basically the same as for cold

weather except for lighter weight selections: long underwear which wicks away perspiration, cotton turtleneck, thin waterproof jacket or wind shirt, waterproof pants. Spring snowboard clothing usually is constructed with zipped underarms on jackets or zippered leg sides on pants which provide venting. Be sure to wear gloves. Lightweight clothing not only protects you from the sun but also from the snow. If you happen to fall, the snow is like sandpaper and the abrasion will be painful on unprotected skin.

Some helmets have warm weather vents, but head coverings, in general, trap the heat. Instead , you can wear a lightweight beany style hat, baseball cap, or headband to look attractive and keep your hair in place while also protecting your ears from sunburn. Sun screen is a must, even for your lip balm. A handy piece of equipment are the hydration packs already mentioned. Dehydration is a problem when on the mountain (particularly in the high altitudes) and easily leads to fatigue, headache, and loss of energy. Leave the fleece clothing at home except do bring something warm for evening wear. I always wonder about the people sitting next to me on a chairlift when the weather is a balmy 50 + degrees, and they are bundled in down jackets. I guess they reasoned that if there is snow on the slopes, then it must be cold out. Not always true.

Rain

For springtime conditions, remember to pack a raincoat. In cold weather it snows, but when temperatures rise, there's rain. Altitude also has bearing on the weather. At Whistler-Blackcomb in British Columbia, Canada, although it can be raining at the lower area of the mountain, it most likely will be snowing in the upper regions.   By the way, snowboarding in the rain is just wonderful. The crowds are sitting indoors at the lodge which means that the trails will be empty of people, and the snow quality tends to be really super. It can be lots of fun, that is **if** you are toasty warm and dry. One important precaution: damp moist air takes away body heat faster than dry air, leaving one vulnerable to chills or even hypothermia. Therefore, although the temperature may be relatively warm, you should remember to dress as if it's actually a bit colder on those damp days.

Appendix :
Products and Where to Find Them

I mentioned the importance of reading the labels, but it is not really quite as simple as that. The problem is twofold: where to find the clothing items in the first place and the fact that each company seems to have a different name for their special "wicking" fabric. Therefore, the following very limited listing (in no particular order) hopefully will be of some help to you in dealing with this quandary.

Hot Chillys

Packaged in funky tin cans ("made and canned in San Luis Obispo, California") are those form fitting tights which I wear as a first base layer, but they have many other snowsport underwear products which range from the moisture wicking fabrics you always want as your first layer closest to your body to fleece tops and bottoms, or their newer items such as the "La Montaña" crop bra which is a one piece combination of fleece shirt and sports bra. www.hotchillys.com.

Patagonia

www.patagonia.com This is a company which specializes in rugged outdoor sportswear. Go to their online store and select "activity," then select "women's snowboarding/skiing," and you will undergo a full education on the movement of moisture through fabric. Their high performance underwear, referred to as "Patagonia Phundamentals," is made of a material which they have developed called "Capilene." There are various products, and the ones you would be interested in would be the Silkweight Stretch (note that silk only refers to the weight, not the fabric), the denser moisture wicking Midweight for greater warmth, or their well known Expedition Weight which is of a super warm fleece. The Web site also explains the concept of layering in three defined zones: Innermost Layer (the moisture wicking fabrics), Insulating Layer (your discretionary decision as to fleece or sweaters), and Outer Layer (jacket or shell).

Burton

Burton has a very strong commitment to women's riding and they even support a Women's Demo Tour. Their product line for the women's market is so extensive that the company publishes a separate catalog just for women. You can go to Burton various ways, either online at www.burton.com , by calling 800-881-3138 to request a catalog, or by seeing the items in person at a quality ski/snowboard shop in your area (check the yellow pages). A pioneer in the industry with their company based in Vermont, the gear is primarily designed for rugged winters. They have a full line of what they refer to as "First Layer Core Weight" items of their Dry Ride 100%

polyester underwear in various weights with the added bonus of being suitable for streetwear. Their years of expertise produce products which are "rider-designed for snowboard-specific performance."

K2

Washington state is at the very opposite coast of the United States from Vermont and the home of K2, another company early involved in the history of snowboarding. Online at www.k2snowboards.com puts you in touch, and their product guide catalog pictures the wide selection of outerwear (along with the expected listings of equipment and accessories), all very specifically designed for our sport. Again, look in your local ski/snowboard shop for these excellent products.

Cold as Ice

Check out the website www.coldasice.com of this company which is just for us girls. They have riding clothing and riding gear (gloves, mitts) and also nifty street clothes. What is sort of special are their "accessories" which include all kinds of wonderful cosmetics such as their "ice kiss lip balm" which not only tastes and feels good on your lips, but also offers SPF-20 protection.

Ski Barn

I live in the New York metropolitan area, and the shop which I go to the most is the Ski Barn, on the web at www.skibarn.com or you can visit any one of their three New Jersey stores (Lawrenceville, Paramus, or Totowa) in person. I have been going to the Totowa store for many years because of their selection of goods and very knowledgeable staff. In fact, I have attended the company's training sessions where staff learns (on snow) about all of the newest product lines for the upcoming season. There's a lot to know to be a savvy salesperson; it requires personal experience with the equipment plus an understanding of the technology. These are qualities to look for to determine where you shop and what you will purchase.

Paragon Sports

For Manhattanites, it seems to me that Paragon Sports has an excellent selection of quality goods. Check them out at 867 Broadway, 212-255-8036 or www.paragonsports.com.

Pelican Sport Center and High Country Sports

New Jersey has many ski clubs and consequently many good shops. Check out Pelican Sport Center, located on Rt. 10 West in Morris Plains, telephone 973-267-0964 or www.pelicanski.com.   Same road, another town and an excellent destination is High Country Sports, 465 Route 10 East, Livingston,973-994-3630, www.hcsports.com

Wild Women Outfitters

Their name says it all. Located in Arlington, MA, you can call them toll free at 1-877-345-WILD or visit at www.wildwomenoutfitters.com.

Snowboarding Clothing Just for Women

Check out the following companies which specialize in

women's only clothing: Betty Rides at www.bettyrides.com, Jewel Wear at jewelwear.com, and Prom which is the women's product line of Swag and Prom at www.snowtraders.com or www.swag.com.

L.L. Bean, REI, E.M.S.

Their website, www.llbean.com offers the full range of catalog items. However, if you go to the "sporting gear and apparel," "Women's sporting apparel," and proceed to then select "skiing & snowboarding," although there are items listed, they certainly are not as technically presented such as with any ski/snowboard shop or compared to, for example, Patagonia. I do recommend, however, the L.L. Bean 100% silk underwear which comes in a Ladies Pointelle Scoop Neck Top (which means that the collar doesn't show under your outer clothing), and their Ladies Silk Long Underwear Bottoms. These are perfect to wear when **not** snowboarding, but, instead, when walking around the ski resort *apres ski* as the sun goes down and temperatures quickly drop.

The list goes on and on, such as the websites for REI (www.rei.com), for E.M.S. (www.easternmountainsports.com), and www.justhersports.com. Certainly, there are other sources available as this book is being written, and more to come, but this will hopefully be a helpful starting point for you.

Helmets

You can't properly purchase a helmet without first trying it on because size is crucial. Heads vary, and a poorly fitting helmet will not only give you a headache but also shortchange you on protection value and even increase your chance of injury. For a listing of your local dealers; contact the companies' Web sites and go shopping on a day when you don't care about your hair getting mussed. Check for lightweight comfort, good hearing ability, ventilation (they can be very hot in the warmer weather and by then you will be addicted to wearing them), and style, of course. According to *Skiing* magazine, the first criteria is that one should definitely only consider those helmets which have passed one of the three safety standards: CE, ASTM, or Snell. The next things to consider are that it should allow good visibility, not be too tight, and be snug enough to not slide around when you move your head up and down. A loose helmet can cause serious neck injury.

Snowboarders tend to wear the "shorty" versions, but really, anything goes. Some popular companies and their sites to check out on the Web are Salomon at www.salomonsports.com, Boeri at www.boeriusa.com, Giro at www.giro.com, Carrera at www.carrerasport.com, and Briko at www.briko.com. WHelmets' team Wendy has a line specifically designed for women, www.whelmets.com. By far and away, however, the best overall Web site to check out is www.lidsonkids.org which will help educate you on the entire subject. Although the name suggests orientation for helmet use by children, there is a great deal of general and very useful information posted here.   The Web site was developed by the National Ski Areas Association, National Ski Patrol, Professional Ski Instructors of America, American Association of Snowboard Instructors, International Brain Injury Association, National Safety Council, and Snowsports Industries America, and is sponsored by Acerbis USA, Boeri, Giro, Leedom, Ovo USA, R.E.D., Salomon, and W Helmets.

Need I say more?

Goggles or Sunglasses

Goggle selection closely follows helmet choice. **Be sure that you are wearing your helmet when selecting goggles.** Otherwise, they simply might not fit. As stated earlier, there is a fairly wide choice of lens color which therefore may require some degree of analysis. According to the Bolle company, Vermillon, their high contrast rose lens is for cloudy/overcast conditions. I find that this lens is excellent in the flat light of late afternoon or on snowy midwinter days. Their Citrus orange is for bright light (sunny) days; Lemon, a yellow, is for low light. Clear lenses are usually only used for night skiing. A single choice could be Phototropic which goes from light amber to dark, depending upon the amount of sunlight.

One might be tempted to purchase one set of goggles with several varied colors of replacement lenses. The problem with this route in terms of my personal experience is that it is not really quite so easy to substitute a lens without cracking it. Goggle replacement lenses are really on the market for when you have to do just that: replace a broken lens, not to do a quick switch based on weather conditions. Investigate the following sites on the Web: www.bolle.com, www.briko.com, www.scott.com, www.carrerasport.com, www.vuarnet.com, www.smith.com, www.gordini.com, www.oakley.com, www.bugz.com, www.spy.com. Because your helmet will hold in body warmth, you should select goggles which have vents, the more the better. Most have top vents, but with helmet usage, the additional front vents make a substantial difference in avoiding fogging. The goggles should fit snugly and be sure that the strap fits properly over the helmet and holds into place.

Sunglasses should also be tried on with your helmet to be sure of comfortable fit. Contact lens users should select frames which either have a wrap around design or have side extending shields, in either case to protect from wind. Look for quality lenses that are shatterproof and will allow you to be out there with full u.v. protection and no squinting. Polarized lenses help cut the harsh glare of sunlight which is amplified by its reflection off of the snow. As with the goggles, some companies even have sunglasses with interchangeable lenses. www.bolle.com, www.zealoptics.com, www.nerveusa.com. , www.oakley.com, www.serengeti.com, www.carrerasport.com, and www.briko.com, are just some of the choices. Select the right lens color. Although they look really cool and funky, those yellow, pink, or red are for low light cloudy conditions. Practically speaking, however, because goggles offer the advantage of wind and cold protection, sunglasses are usually reserved for warmer weather which means that it is usually bright and sunny, so choose your lens color accordingly.

Remember that unlike the fashion market for street wear, in snowsports country the price is your best indication of lens quality and impact protection.

Socks

I have already mentioned the importance of wearing a good athletic sock and recommend the Thorlo company which makes different socks for a variety of sporting activities, including snowboarding. Their snowboard sock has cushioning in just the right places: www.thorlo.com or call 888 t-h-o-r-l-o-s for the nearest retailer.

Resort Area Snowboard Shops

In truth, almost all of my equipment purchases are made either, as already stated, at my local ski shop in the town where I live or at my resort. I work at Killington where the company resort ski stores are Chrisports Ski Shops, and Shops at the Shack, both carrying high quality goods. Along with these I recommend several of my local snowboard shops: Out of Bounds snowboard shop, www.ridevt.com , or First Stop-Board Barn at www.info@firststopski.com. The advantage of these ski area shops is that they can devote their stock to exclusively handle only snowboarding products. If you know what you want, it's just a matter of your finding the shop with that item in its inventory. Really, the very best way to shop is in person so that you can try on things, and the very best place to shop is either at your home located specialty ski/snowboard shop or at those of your destination resort. There is one problem with ski area shopping which is that although the resort stores may be numerous and usually excellent, including those run by the ski area itself, however, a person simply has limited time (and energy) to go shopping after a day on the slopes. But, this is a great place to pick up exactly the item you have been seeking, that is if you have the strength to muster up for the shopping expedition! It's not the snowboarding lesson itself that is so tiring but the use of new muscles plus the day long exposure to the outdoors. It can be exhausting.

Which source did I forget? Perhaps the biggest and the best!

An indefatigable resource is www.snowlink.com which really is the penultimate source for all listings! Here you will find the websites for equipment, clothing, resort information, snowsport articles, weather reports for resort areas, lesson information, just about everything you never even thought you could have wanted to know!

3

On Fear of Injury and Fear Itself

The second element of snowboarding which women seem most concerned with, after the "What will I wear and where can I get it?" problem has been settled, is dealing with fear of injury. I have developed a habit of asking details of people who have been hurt. Their answers always reveal the same category of inappropriate activity: going onto a trail which was above their ability level (often due to the coaxing of so-called friends who insist "you can do it"), deciding to attempt snowboarding without taking a lesson, disregarding instruction, learning to snowboard from a friend rather than someone professionally trained in instructing, *etc.* Yes, there is always the element of bad luck, but usually the stage is set by one of the above situations. The bottom line is that you should take a lesson with a professional, predicated on the assumption that the quality of instruction is high at your selected ski resort.

Is snowboarding safer than skiing? That is really the question. I, personally, had decided to stop skiing and instead take up snowboarding because of two previous skiing falls wherein my knee had been somewhat twisted resulting in injury. Realizing that this type of twist could never happen on

Snowboarding for Women

a snowboard as both feet are locked onto the board and one leg cannot travel in the opposite direction to the other, I decided that it would be the safer snowsport for me. Torn knee ligaments are skiing's major area of injury. Later confirmed by my orthopaedist, my decision to switch to snowboarding was a wise one.

You may be aware of the fact that female athletes face a higher risk than do men of tearing knee ligaments, specifically the ACL, which is the critical ligament for holding the knee together. There have been numerous studies as to the explanation of why women have four to six times the risk that men face, with as numerous the theories, some of which conclude that female hormones may be a factor. Other theories accuse the weaker muscular system of women as well as male-female skeletal differences. The definite causes have not yet been proven, but the fact remains that we are certainly more vulnerable than men are.

When skiing women are asked about trying snowboarding, they tend to express apprehension at the prospect of having both feet in locked position on the board. Their nervousness is predicated upon a false concept of safety. The firm attachment of both feet is a better way to avoid knee injury. As stated, this was the decision I had made in my own case and the one I advise for other women. I truly believe that snowboarding is safer than skiing. This view was reaffirmed recently when I accompanied my skier husband to his sport medicine orthopaedic doctor to discuss the torn meniscus in his knee. The doctor advised him not to ski but instead to snowboard citing the aforementioned fact that the snowboarder does not risk that injurious twisting wrench to the knee. My reason for initially taking up snowboarding was now officially

Chapter 3 On Fear of Injury and Fear Itself

stated and endorsed by a medical expert.

The most common snowboard injury is to the wrist, caused by the person reaching out with arm extended to prevent falling. Instead of the broken fall, the result is often a broken wrist!   There are snowboard gloves with built in wrist protectors and some people use in-line skating wrist guards, but I am not in favor of either option for several reasons. One is that they are awkward, making it difficult to adjust bindings or do other fine motions. The second reason is because the shock of impact is then merely transferred to the next joint, the elbow. Look at your wrist. It is absurd to expect this body joint to support the thrust of your entire body. It is simply much easier to keep hands pulled to the body, and, if feeling a loss of balance, just sit down. Never reach out to brace yourself from a fall.

I recently attended a symposium on ski and snowboard injuries with a presentation by Ann Stein, M.D., of the Vermont Orthopaedic Clinic, who is board certified in both General Orthopaedics and Hand Surgery. She also asserted the negative effects of wearing wrist guards, although she wears them herself. After the talk I told her that I encourage my clinic participants to wear knee pads, thus developing an automatic reaction of dropping to the knees without hesitation when off balance. She found this to be an interesting solution to the problem of reaching out with arm extended to break a fall and mused that when she learned to ski she had been taught how to fall. Apparently, I had given her food for thought.

A second possible injury risk area is the tail bone. I've personally never fallen backward onto my tail bone, but many people complain of such an injury. A very simple solution for protection would be to take a washcloth or guest towel folded into a small square and positioned inside your long underwear. Burton has a product, the Burton Impact Short, which has padded protection for the tail bone and hips. There are several such snowboarding specific items now on the market. These are similar to what boys who play football refer to as a "girdle," available at neighborhood sporting goods stores. I have recommended this item, particularly when I am working with someone who is disabled and at high risk in terms of injury.

I once gave a snowboard lesson to a person who enthusiastically believed in protective padding. He wore all of the standard in-line skating gear of helmet, elbow pads, knee pads, and wrist guards, plus pants which were designed with strips of padding on the upper thighs. When asked if he was afraid of injury (which certainly seemed to be an understatement), his reply was not what I'd expected. "How could I possibly get hurt with all this protection?" was his optimistic answer. He had no fear of injury and therefore was easily able to concentrate on his new learning experience. This is an extreme case, and such extensive equipment is rather cumbersome, but perhaps there is something to be said about this approach. If you address your fears, then you may actually eliminate them.

Several years ago I attended a snowboard camp and found myself in a reverse position in that I was among the students rather than in the role of instructor. I was absolutely astounded at the confessions of my fellow classmates in their descriptions of extensive padding to prevent injury. They wore hockey shoulder pads, knee pads, football tailbone pads.... You name it, they padded it! Again, if there is no fear of injury, one is less tentative, leading to a more positive performance, and the fact that snowboard clothing is so loose enables one to discreetly pad to excess.

Other than tailbone padding (although I've never personally done so), the only thing that I really recommend is the use of knee pads, preferably the kind used in telemark skiing as these are soft and designed for use on snow. Roofers' knee pads, gardening pads, or the ones from in-line skating will also do. The reason for knee pads is because snowboarders spend a lot of time either sitting or kneeling. When kneeling, your knees get really cold. As mentioned in the clothing section, snowboard pants often are constructed with inside pockets for foam pad inserts at the knee. It does not require serious dressmaking skills to do it yourself in sewing patch pockets inside the knee areas of your outerwear pants. In terms of injury protection, inserted pads will cushion your knees from impact and, perhaps equally importantly, from the cold. As earlier mentioned in regard to my conversation with Dr. Ann Stein, I have found that when wearing knee pads there was no hesitation to drop to my knees the moment I felt off balance, thus eliminating the reflex of reaching out with wrist extended or falling onto one's shoulder. Padded knees are definitely the single most important requisite for both body protection and general comfort and particularly important to have for that first lesson.

Absolutely to be considered in the category of safety is the wearing of a helmet. I had already been wearing a helmet for several years when celebrity ski deaths focused a great deal of attention on the subject of helmet safety. It is not really determined whether helmets would have prevented death in the cases of Sonny Bono or Michael Kennedy, both of whom struck trees. According to an article in the Winter 1998 issue of *The Professional Skier* (published by PSIA, Professional Ski

Snowboarding for Women

Instructors of America) entitled "Helmets Gain Popularity in Snowsports Industry" by Julie K. Hall, helmets offer protection "from impact with a stationary object at 12 miles per hour...[and] skiers involved in fatal collisions are generally skiing faster than that." If this subject makes you really nervous, however, you can put the risk factor into perspective. According to Jim Russell, M.D., of the Killington Medical Clinic, head injuries in winter sports account for 2.5% of all injuries, as opposed to 5% in soccer, 87% in professional boxing, 10% in college football, and 20% high school football. Remember that last number when your son asks to play high school football!

Nevertheless, wearing a helmet does offer protection from and reduce the severity of concussions. I once had a major crash while snowboarding(in all honesty, my only one ever of its kind, but once was enough). I was feeling overconfident and certainly going too fast when I lost my balance, leaned back (oh, no!), and must have resembled a cartoon character whose head was going *boingg boingg* as it bounced on the snow. Also I have seen skiers and snowboarders alike who crash their heads on lift chairs or are bashed in the head by ski toting resort guests. The helmet offers excellent protection from such dangers. An added bonus for me is the fact that on those days of extreme wind chill, the helmet keeps your head toasty warm.

If all this talk has frightened you, a *Wall Street Journal* article of January 12, 1998, pointed out that safety and sound judgement are the important factors in terms of mountain safety and head injuries. The article quotes Terence Davidson, professor of surgery at the University of California at San Diego and a 30 year veteran of the Mammoth Mountain Ski

Chapter 3 On Fear of Injury and Fear Itself

Patrol, who states that most impact injuries are not really skiing/snowboarding accidents, but instead occur by those persons who "happened to be on skis while doing something stupid." See the listing of helmet products in the Appendix area of Chapter 2.

I would **not** advise anyone to snowboard who has a bad back. The risk of doing damage outweighs the positive experience of having fun snowboarding. For those who like to wear fanny packs or backpacks, if you do this while snowboarding, you may wind up with a bad back, so leave those items in the locker.

The point of all this is not to frighten anyone, but it is unrealistic to assume that we are immune to injury. Snowboarding does have its risks, although I have always maintained that it is safer than skiing. Wrist bones heal, whereas the skier's knee injury of a torn ligament requires complicated surgery. Also, a most important aspect of injury prevention is personal conditioning. Although at my ski area we like to believe that within the on-snow time of our standard group lesson you can learn to snowboard, this is based on the presumption that the guest is in reasonable physical condition. Lower expectation should be made for couch potatoes who never take part in any physical activity, for those who are exhausted after the long drive from home to the ski area the previous night which resulted in less than their normal hours of sleep, and for those who were out partying with alcohol consumption causing an element of dehydration. All of these factors contribute toward the risk of injury. Be practical about this adventure, and give it your best effort by proper preparation in terms of general conditioning.

The problem with fear is not always due to its origins.

Snowboarding for Women

Some fears are realistically conceived, others falsely; nevertheless, perception is reality. This means that if you **think** that something is dangerous or frightening, it simply **is.** Logical explanation has no role here. A result of fear is often a physical one in that muscles tense up. Your fear, which has sent a message of "I know that I can't do that"or " I know that I will be hurt,"results in a stiffening of body muscles which guarantees a sort of wish fulfillment of your assertion in that you certainly will not be able to make the proper moves. What does one do with such a head case? Just avoid the situation where fear is in the driver's seat. Stay with a qualified instructor and build your confidence based on the reality of your skill level.

An often stated fear is that of heights. Women tend to voice this phobia at the very mention of setting foot on the ski/snowboard resort scene. First of all, as a beginner at most resorts you usually will not be going high up on the mountain as the terrain would tend to be too steep for your ability level. Secondly, there are various ways to deal with the tendency to have vertigo. One looks straight ahead, not down, to avoid that sinking feeling. Or, don't look out at all! Your instructor will guide you in lift usage (see Chapter 9 for specifics on how to take a chairlift), and there are other options of lift systems which are either enclosed or on the ground surface .

That was always one of my biggest fears: how could I become a ski instructor if I had a fear of heights? I've kept my eyes squeezed shut many times, particularly in Europe, asking my chair partner when it was safe to open them and getting a running report of the spectacular sights I was missing! It's not really a big deal. If I could work it out, anyone can.

Chapter 3 On Fear of Injury and Fear Itself

FEAR, in capital letters

It's a funny thing with fear. Fear can create a certain degree of tension and anxiety which may be an asset. You are pushing yourself to achieve and conquer your fear with a result of intense exhilaration at your success. On the other hand, fear can create paralysis. Muscles and joints go rigid, and you absolutely are no longer physically capable of enacting the moves you know you should make. The first way to deal with such fear is simply to avoid these situations. Do not join friends going to places which you know will be beyond your skill level. When your lesson ends, be sure to ask your instructor which areas on the mountain would be appropriate for your skill level. Remember that trails tend to get "skied off" in the late afternoon which means that the snow surface has become slick. This is due to the fact that by now softer snow has been pushed aside due to the accumulation of skier traffic over the course of the day.   Changing light and afternoon shadows causing vision difficulty plus drops in temperature are additional factors to be considered. Fatigue is another element.   I never take a "last run" but instead stop the previous run before I am too tired to really enjoy it fully.

New riders tend to become tense and fearful when on a busy trail. Basic insecurities come to the fore as one not only has to contend with the elements of riding skills, but also there is the worry that someone else will be lacking in their own skills and crash into us. For some reason, people seem to come clumped in waves of groups down a trail. The best advice is to go to the side, out of the way, and wait a moment until things quiet down, and then you can regain your concentration and composure. Remember that the sound of the snowboard can also create fearful situations for others. That is why it helps to

Snowboarding for Women

call out "on your right" or "on your left" to the person you are overtaking. Taking control of a situation can help reduce your own fear factor as you find your way through the crowds.

Some coaches advise singing while you ride. Song helps in that it relaxes you and also induces rhythm which will remind you to even out your turns (we all tend to hold onto or favor one direction of a turn longer than the other). Nervousness can actually cause you to unconsciously hold your breath. Counter this tendency by doing some deep breathing. Smiling also helps, as does self-imaging. Focus on how well you are doing, rather than worrying about what is ahead. I always tell my students to stop and look back. See how far you have come, and be impressed that it was over such challenging terrain. Instead of being your worst critic, try being your own fan club, and give yourself some pats on the back.

No matter how experienced or advanced a rider we are, there is always a place or circumstance which can unnerve us. We become frozen, unable to initiate a move! Here is where imaging and the power of positive thinking come into use. Imagine how you would *like* to ride this trail; creating a mental picture will help lead the way. Take it in small portions in that you need not do the entire distance. Instead, just deal with a limited number of turns to go part way. Then tackle the remainder. One reason why this situation may arise is the fact that seeing a line of skiers or boarders all stopped at the height of a trail has the power of suggesting to you that something horrendous is ahead, out of sight but just over the ridge. Resist the urge of stopping in their company not only because their fear is contagious, but also because you would have lost your rhythm which makes it hard to begin again. Pass through the crowd, proceeding   with due caution, but proceeding nevertheless.

The key to controlling fear is to have confidence. The way to have confidence is to build upon success, and the road to success is "mileage." Work and rework those basic skills with miles of experience on appropriately challenging terrain before adventuring to a higher level of difficulty. As to the reputation of the first snowboarding lesson as a punishing experience, I honestly believe in a "no-crash" lesson. That applies to my group clinics along with the private lessons. It really is not necessary to have first time snowboarders flying out of control and crashing; that is not a positive reinforcement method of learning. Instead, a good coach will guide the group in a sequence of maneuvers which are success oriented. The true problem is in identifying that "good coach."

One method is to check on AASI accreditation. This refers to the American Association of Snowboard Instructors, a national organization which certifies its members in levels of accomplishment which refer not only to skill at snowboarding, but more importantly to the resort guest, the organization evaluates teaching techniques and understanding of the sport's technology. All of this means that if you see a Level I pin, you know that the instructor is associated. If there is a Level II jacket pin, the person has passed a three day exam testing technological understanding, teaching, and riding ability. With Level III comes recognition of the highest accreditation in the mastering of the organization's standards. At least the awareness of AASI offers you some guide as to competence, and the better your instructor, the more you will learn, the more confident you will become, and the less fear you will carry with you to inhibit your skill level and lessen your enjoyment of the total experience of snowboarding.

Snowboarding for Women

The point of this chapter is **not** to instill fear of injury but rather to allay fears by confronting the reality that sports involve risks. You will certainly be safer sitting home, but is that really what life is all about? Being with friends and family is certainly more stimulating than sitting staring at a television screen in emotional isolation. Snowboarding offers an escape from everyday matters with the excitement of getting away. It brings you out with friends, providing a socially interactive experience. Its outdoor activity refreshes and invigorates your life. All of these positive factors far outweigh the negatives of injury risk, especially when the latter is, to a very great extent, within your control. Accidents happen, but people do tend to play a role in causing them. Safety awareness and caution are keys to returning home happy and injury free.

Hi,
my name is
Betty Shred,
and
I'm just
thrilled that
you
wannabe
like me!
Now that the problem of clothing has been taken care of and we've dealt with that nasty subject of fear...

Let's get going!

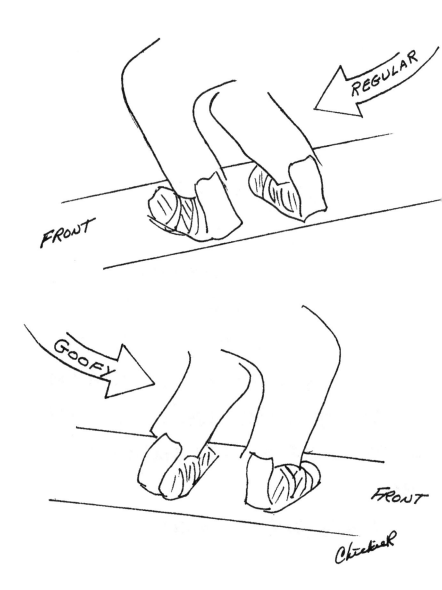

4
Life is Full of Decisions: Regular or GOOFY

It's decided. You intend to snowboard, you have the proper duds, and you know fully what you are getting into, but when you enter a snowboard rental shop whether at your hometown or the resort, the question will be the same: "Do you ride regular or goofy?"

This refers to the orientation of your front foot on the snowboard. The right foot forward is referred to as *goofy*, a term from surfing; left foot forward is called *regular* due to the fact that most people are left oriented. Burton suggests that its shops set up boards anticipating a ratio of 65 to 35, regular to goofy footed. It is a somewhat crucial choice but often overstated. When I was so very poorly coordinated during my first snowboarding attempt, I swore it was because I had selected the wrong foot forward. A quick trip to rental with an equipment exchange proved even more disastrous; it was the driver, not the vehicle.

Here is what this is all about. Unlike the frontal position when skiing, snowboarders employ a sideways stance which is determined by **putting the weight bearing leg foremost** on the board. The problem arises in determining which foot takes that front position. This has absolutely nothing to do with being right or left handed. Remember that.

If you have skateboarded or surfed, you will assume that same stance on the snowboard. If you have a weak leg or one which has suffered previous injury, you do <u>not</u> want it in the forward binding. Snowboard pros have various techniques for determining the frontal leg, most of them totally unscientific. Some use an eyesight dominance test which I have never understood. Others like to sneak up upon the unsuspecting person with a strong push, watching to see which leg goes forward first, thus interpreting it as the stronger one. Another popular method of determining which leg goes in front involves simulating sliding across a slippery floor. The forward sliding foot is the forward snowboarding foot. I find all of the above to be less than accurate.

Perhaps the best test is simply to ask yourself which foot you would use to kick a ball, remember that in such a situation, your body weight is balanced on the <u>non</u> kicking foot. Therefore <u>that stationary foot, not the kicking foot,</u> is your choice for frontal position. There is another test you could try, since you know of this in advance as you read these lines in the comfort of your home. Be conscious of your body as you stand around talking on the telephone, brushing your teeth, doing the dishes, folding laundry. Which leg do you seem to favor with most of your weight? That is your forward foot.

Other than applying the kicking a ball test, I like to use a different method, although it is certainly less easy to explain its validity. I really don't know why, but it seems to work. Fold your arms across your chest. Women are more

Chapter 4 Life is Full of Decisions

accustomed to this arm position than men are, so it seems to be a more reliable technique with them.   Which is the outermost arm? If left, then you are left foot forward; right arm outer should result in right foot forward. It is usually as simple as that.   Ultimately, if you are still unsure, go with left foot forward. The very fact that this position is called "regular" should direct the undecided to accept that determination for their own initial riding experience. Remember that <u>it has absolutely nothing to do with being right or left handed.</u> Once you have decided your body orientation, do not belabor the point.   Do not agonize over your decision. Stick with your choice and do not doubt it. **Do not let anyone talk you out of it!**

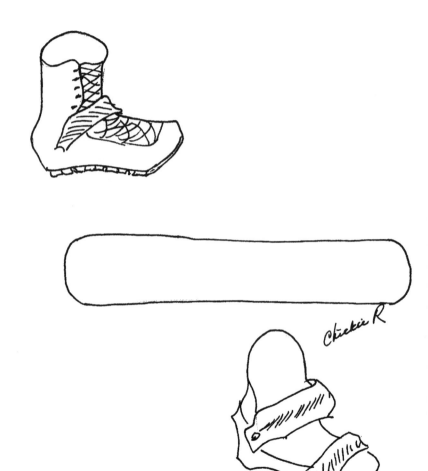

Chickie R

5

The Three B's--
Boots, Boards, and
Bindings

Entering a snowboard rental shop can be a harrowing experience if you are not prepared in terms of the various choices you will be making. Note that the focus of this chapter is on rental selection to guide you through that first initial equipment set up, rather than being a buyer's guide. For advice on purchasing, Chapter 11 has the in depth approach on equipment which will make you a wise consumer. If you are planning on going that route, be sure to read this earlier chapter carefully as a preface to the more technical analysis which will come later.

Boots

There are soft boots, and there are hard boots. Although skiers are somewhat naturally inclined to prefer the hard version because of their familiarity with a hard shell boot, that choice of boot also bears similarity to ski boots in its level of discomfort and lack of warmth.   And don't even think about using your ski boots for snowboarding! Their flex pattern design is all wrong for boarding, and they won't fit properly into the binding. Then who should use hard boots? Hard boot systems are on the market for riders who want to race. This is life in the fast lane and certainly not the equipment suitable for a first time beginner. People often insist on going the hard boot route, but it is has been obvious to me over years of instructing that **it is very difficult to learn snowboarding in hard boots.** Do not create a handicap for yourself before you even go out onto the snow.

Soft boots offer the advantages of comfort, warmth, and ease of walking. Their design has been created for general riding which is referred to in boot sales marketing as *all mountain* and also for what is called *freestyle* which is for doing tricks and use in a snowboard park or half pipe. Try them on and select what is comfortable for you, the same as you would for any other sport shoe (keeping in mind the advice in Chapter 2 regarding socks). Boots should be snug enough to prevent excessive heel lift but large enough that your toes lie flat and relaxed on the footbed.

When you are sitting down putting on the boots it is okay if your toes seem to brush the front of the boot lining because usually when you stand up and bend your knees the lining will then stretch and your heel and toes will move back. If one size does not fit, dependent upon the rental shop's inventory, you can often ask for the same size but a different manufacturer. Also, you may have a choice of *step-ins* which refers to a boot specifically partnered with its binding arrangement, although this will create other concerns (see section on bindings).

You have been told to only wear one sock layer, and it

should be a sturdy sport sock, no stockings. A problem you will encounter is that your long underwear will come down into the boot area, causing bulk and chaffing. What you must do is pull the bottom edge of the underwear cuff up onto the calf area of the leg with flattened folds. Stirrups must also be treated this way. If you have planned ahead, you will have done this before coming to the rental shop and might even have cut the underwear to shorten its length. If not, then it is something else to deal with as you try on boots. The only thing to enter the boot should be your foot and its sock covering.

While on the subject of boots, it is important to remember that feet perspire, and your boots will be quite damp by the end of the day. If you are planning to wear them again tomorrow, be sure that you store them overnight in a warm place (not left in the car trunk).   Open them up to insure air circulation and even consider using a hair dryer set on low to carefully enhance drying . I say "carefully," because it is easy to either overheat the boot interior or cause a problem with the hair dryer itself. There are many excellent products sold at ski shops which are specifically designed to dry ski or snowboard boots. If you are considering making such a purchase, you should select boot dryers which are portable as they will be an additional item on your snowboard trip packing list.

BOARDS

Snowboards are measured in centimeter lengths and the rental shop will guide you in the selection of the appropriate size dependent upon your height, weight, and ability level. There are boards designed specifically for women, but don't anticipate that these will be available in the rental inventory, although it should definitely be a factor for your consideration when it comes to making an equipment purchase.

Some resort snowboard schools are using special boards not available for the public purchasing market which have been designed specifically for teaching beginners. They are less rigid, having softer flex and, to aid in the teaching process, edges are beveled to help avoid the sudden sharp losses of balance so upsetting to the novice (the dreaded "snowboarder's slam"). You can ask the rental shop if this is an option available to you.

Be sure to cite your experience level whether going out for the first time as a "never-ever" or having had limited previous experience. The length and even style choice of your snowboard is predicated upon ability level and where you will be riding (race course, park, or all mountain). Height and weight are additional factors. *Snowboarder Magazine* uses a formula of multiplying your height (in inches) times 2.54 times 0.9 to determine board length in cm's. Rather than bringing along a calculator, you can usually place confidence in the rental shop to supply you with the proper board. Trust them; that's their business.

Since you are reading this book, and thus far Chapter 5 rather than Chapter 11, then you are too much of a novice to consider the alpine racing board at this stage of your snowboarding experience, so there will not be a discussion of the subject here. Anyway, you should have been convinced that hard boots are not the best starting set up for the beginner.

The all mountain or free riding boards can work fine doing park and pipe, but usually spend most of their riding time on regular mountain trails. These are the boards best suited for your first time out, and resort rental shops have a wide inventory to assure proper match for your needs, provided that you make arrangements in enough time before their resources are depleted. Go early for the least hassle and the best selection.

Bindings

Hard boots require *plate* bindings. Be careful not to catch your fingers under the clamps, but hopefully I have discouraged you in this equipment choice when you are just starting out.

There are two options for soft boot bindings. The first entails a setup with either two or sometimes three straps. The three strap offers the most support as there is one across the upper foot, one over the instep area, and the third over the toes. The problem with three straps is that there are too many straps to deal with each time you step in or out of the binding, hence the more popular and practical design is that of a two strap binding. These usually ratchet, are easy to work, and only have the disadvantage of requiring a deep exercise bend each time buckling or unbuckling is necessary.

On the other hand, a step-in system frees you from crouching down to buckle, eliminates the clumsiness of working buckles with mittened hands, and will allow you to be first in the group ready and set to go. A complication is that this necessitates a companion boot to the specific system (*ie.* K-2 boots go with the Clicker system, *etc.*) which means that your choice must be predicated upon the comfortable fit of the required boot. As to the binding itself, nothing is trouble free. Ice tends to adhere and harden around the metal connection areas and soft snow clumps, at times making it difficult to do an easy step-in.

Important: note that there is a shield like plastic piece, some eight inches or so high which protrudes perpendicular to the rear of the binding. This is called a *highback*. Some step-in systems have placed the highbacks inside of their boots which means that the boot has a stiff backing from the heel up to the top, making it uncomfortable for walking. The better choice is to select a step-in where the highback is external as part of the binding system which is located on the board rather than inside the boot.

How to decide between the convenience of a step-in versus straps? For the beginning snowboarder it is a decision weighing the advantage of a quick-to-ready position as opposed to the definite problem which exists in terms of understanding how to balance when out on the mountain slope with the forward foot already locked into position. It is a challenge not to fall over while placing the back foot into its binding or struggling to clear clogged up snow from the mechanism. This maneuver can be very tricky. Most shops only offer the buckle system for rentals, so you probably won't even have a choice initially. You can make a decision which is best for you later on when you are more experienced and are deciding on purchasing your own gear.

Binding Settings

There are several binding adjustments, all of which are referred to as "stance," and these should be checked out before embarking on your great adventure. Modifications are important as the previous renter most likely would have been a person with a very different body structure from yours.

(1) The shop technician can move the bindings closer together or farther apart. Stand on the board and be sure that

your feet are a comfortable distance apart. According to the manufacturing companies, technically, stance should be determined by the measurement of distance from the ground to the back of the knee. Not in the habit of carrying a tape measure, I have instead simply approximated the shoulder to shoulder width distance and used this measure for how far apart your feet should be. In fact, I just measured my own body, and the knee-floor number is the same as my shoulder to shoulder measurement, so I guess that is why the system of approximation works just fine.

(2) The technician can also make a second area of adjustment which involves stance angle. There is a disk which shows degree of foot direction slant marked in 3 degree intervals, with zero being straight across the middle of the board, equator like. The higher the angle number, the more the foot is tilted toward the front of the board, therefore the more suitable for advanced or aggressive riders. Thus, for never-ever snowboarders, I suggest a stance for beginners of anywhere from 15 to 23 degrees for the front foot, and at least 8 degrees less for the back foot. For example, try 20° for the front foot and 9° for the back, or set at 15° for the front foot with 6° for the back foot. Determine which appears to be more comfortable when the knees are gently bent. Often boards are seen with that back foot set to zero which puts a great deal of unpleasant pressure and subsequent discomfort on rear leg muscles. Another problem with the back foot set to zero is that it becomes very difficult to bend both knees.

Lately, for no apparent reason, I've been having people come for lessons with their feet set in what we call *duck foot*. The front foot points outward in typical degree angle, but the back foot has the same degree angle in a negative sense, pointing in the opposite direction. This is a really functional set up for those people doing free style spins and tricks, because the rider wants to be comfortable going in both directions, forward or backward (*switch*). The disadvantage for a person new to snowboarding is that with feet pointing outward, ballerina style, it is very difficult to assume a flexed knee stance. When learning, you need all the help you can get, and hindering yourself with awkward binding angles is a definite handicap.

(3) Bindings can also be moved for placement towards the front or rear of the board. If you are in the East, I am sure they will have been set slightly back of the center, but if out West and on a heavy powder day, it is preferable to be much more to the rear. Presumably, the shop will have anticipated that, but it's good to mention as it not only shows that you are knowledgeable but that you care.

(4) Bindings are also adjustable in terms of the board width. Check to be sure that your heels or toes do not extend over the width (side edges) of the board edge. This is referred to as toe or heel drag which has the negative effect similar to if you are trying to go full sail on a boat while simultaneously dragging an anchor. The problem is more common with men who have large boot sizes, and extra wide boards are available for such situations. Although board width is not usually a concern for women, it is still another reason to use the freestyle soft boot set up rather than the hard boot as the latter is combined with a skinny race board thereby forcing the rider into a more angled (and aggressive) riding position in order to

avoid boot drag.

Accessories

The board should have a *leash* and a *stomp pad.* The leash is a prehensile body part of the original snowboard binding design. In the early years of riding it acted as a safety strap to keep the board from soaring loose if the binding opened up, but today's bindings neither release without manipulation nor tear out of their drilled holes, yet the safety rules at mountains still require leash employment to the point that their lift operators will stop you if the leash is not present or attached.

The second item, a stomp pad, is important because it provides a skid proof surface for the back foot to rest upon when not buckled into the binding. This is either a mat or some sort of rough surfaced device. If either of these accessories are not on the board, be sure to request them. Having a good stomp pad can make a serious difference in your ability to exit successfully from a chairlift.

Where to Rent

A decision must be made in terms of where to rent your equipment. Certainly, it is easier to rent at your home neighborhood where you have the advantage of time and place, as opposed to the crowds lined up all rushing to make the lesson on time when at the resort rental shop. However, the main advantage of renting at the ski/snowboard resort facility (and this is a very serious advantage) is the flexibility of the situation. If you have a problem such as a strap breaking (which often happens as a result of frigid temperatures), if the board is the wrong size, if there is a problem with the binding, *etc.*, all you need do is go to rental and get an exchange. If the equipment is from an outside source, you are stuck with it. Another reason to rent at the resort mountain shop is because most ski areas offer special price breaks for lift, lesson and equipment packages. Those savings can actually be quite major. Beware, however, that if you plan on doing a resort rental, allow ample time to do so and go early anyway, because it seems as if there are never enough boards for all the people who arrive determined to take up the sport.

Summary

In case you are feeling overloaded with information, here is a checklist of what you should do when selecting board, boots, and bindings:

* Say that you are a beginner.
* Be sure to state whether you are goofy or regular.
* Wear a sturdy sock without liner or stockings underneath.
* Ask for soft boots which should fit comfortably without the heel drastically slipping up. There may be a little play, but not more than about a half inch (Do not expect the form fit of a ski boot).
* Ask for an all mountain board suitable for your size and weight.
* Check how far apart your feet are set and if your stance feels comfortable; know the binding angles and watch out for toe drag.
* Be sure that there is a leash and stomp pad.

Do Not Leave the Rental Shop Without being sure that
YOU KNOW HOW TO WORK THE BINDINGS
YOUR BOOT FITS PROPERLY INTO THE BINDING PLATE
YOU CAN CLOSE THE BINDING STRAPS
YOU ARE SET WITH THE CORRECTLY DESIGNATED FORWARD FOOT

As we said earlier, looking good is most of the game. Therefore, to look like a pro as you leave the shop, you should carry the board under your arm, smooth surface inside next to your body, nose (front tip) pointing upward. Take care to wear gloves as the board edges can be very sharp. **You're now on your way!!!!**

SNOWBOARD
CLINICS
MEET HERE

6
Lesson Introduction

This chapter is absolutely not intended to be a substitute for an actual live, on the snow, in person, at the mountain, lesson. To learn snowboarding from a book would be akin to learning to dance with neither partner nor music. The better use of this "lesson introduction" would be to advise you on what to expect and even to help enact preparatory simulated movements which you can do in your home or hotel room environment, all in anticipation of your upcoming snowboard professionally coached lesson. By the way, notice that I have underscored "professionally coached." Friends can't teach friends how to snowboard. Knowing how to ride does not mean knowing how to teach riding. Professional snowboard instructors are not only experienced in what they do, but often receive additional training at their mountain plus maintaining active membership in a national organization, the American Association of Snowboard Instructors (AASI), whose membership requires attendance at instructional teaching clinics.

Upon going outdoors (and you can do this indoors if you are reading and simulating the experience), the first thing I have clinic participants do is to place the board face down on the snow surface. There is a optimal way to do everything. The correct way is to set down the board with its bindings on

87

the snow. Beware; if resting with the base on snow, the board may suddenly take off sliding downhill, and you will be frantically chasing after it. Create good habits from the outset.

Since many snowboarder hopefuls have had an experience skiing, I ask people (with snowboards safely put aside) to assume the skier's posture. This means that one faces front, knees slightly bent, hands forward as if holding imaginary ski poles. Next, make your legs knock-kneed. Then, place a hand on the knee of the leg which has the (previously determined) forward position on the board . This is to remind you <u>not</u> to move that leg. Place the other leg parallel behind so that you are now standing angled somewhat sideways, both knees slightly bent. You have now assumed a simulated stance position as if your feet would be locked into the snowboard bindings. Your head should be up and looking forward, although the trunk of your body has twisted sideways. Yes, it's a weird and awkward body position.

Now for the important part. As the kids say: "Listen up!" For beginners, **the golden rule of snowboarding is weight on the front foot.** Later on, as you become more advanced, your weight will be shifted, but, for now, it is, I repeat, **weight on the front foot.** To be more precise, one really is placing <u>most</u> weight on the front foot; if you adhere to the command of <u>all weight</u> you might simply topple forward!

Kinesthetics refers to awareness of your body and noticing how things "feel." To create sensitivity and kinesthetic response to your stance, there are two important movements which I have people enact. Here you are, standing with both hands comfortably forward, and you are looking ahead. Be aware of the fact that your weight is placed on the front foot. Next, instead of continuing to look up and ahead, look down at your feet. Now-- where is your weight? Notice that your balance has shifted, and you are now standing with weight on your back foot. Try this several times, and, if with a friend doing it together, you will actually see the weight shift happening in conjunction with altered direction of view. Why is this important? If you are snowboarding and look down at your feet or focus on the snow under your path of movement, your weight will have shifted from the front to the rear of the board which, as will be shown, can have disastrous consequences. Test your body stance and the corresponding weight transfers until you are truly conscious of your body movements and their resultant effect upon balance.

A snowboard is designed to travel forward with your body weight pressuring towards the front end. That was one of the reasons why you had determined at the outset which would be your weight bearing forward foot. Therein is the crucial fact. If you weight the rear of the board, one of two things will happen. Either the board will react as if the rear is the front, spin around 180,° and send you downhill completely backwards, or, in a worse case scenario, the backward weight onto the tail of the board will cause you to resemble the silhouette of a speedboat with front end up in the air as you jet out of control with a forward lurch.

The lesson to be learned is actually rather simple. The ideal body position for the first time learner is to be comfortably balanced with weight dispersed approximately 70% front foot, 30% back, arms hanging at your side which means that the trailing arm is towards the back foot (remember that your stance is sideways, not frontal, on the board). However, if you feel that you are losing balance, simply remember to increase weight on the front foot, and, for extra safety, lift your arms forward (as if holding a tray). Arms and shoulders are heavy; therefore, because you have brought that trailing arm forward in an emergency move, you have added stabilizing weight to the front which will quickly reassert your balance. Do note that body position itself is always in flux, never frozen into a rigid stance; however, it is helpful to be aware of the optimal position for balance. It will come in handy.

Your general stance should be an athletic one with knees relaxed into a slightly bent position and ankles flexed. Don't forget to smile. Are you aware that smiling relaxes the body and also helps create a sense of well being? Another reason to smile is because you are out there to have fun!

Now you are *finally* ready to buckle your front foot onto the board. Standing with the heel of your free (destined-to-be back) foot on snow bracing you, with the toe of that boot holding the board steady, place your other (front) foot into the binding and buckle up. Place the <u>front foot only</u> into its binding. Do the upper strap first, then the toe strap. The newer systems simply require insertion and then ratcheting to attain a snug fit. The boot should be firmly held in place to avoid shifting but not so tight as to cut off blood circulation. Next, connect the leash which either goes around the ankle or snaps into the boot lace.

Slightly lift up the board into the air, and feel how it is a clumsy weight. Put it back down, and tilt it to slide on the edges, toe side then heel side, in a sawing motion going back and forth, cutting lines into the snow (be careful if your practice session of these moves is on carpeting as your snowboard's edges can be extremely sharp and therefore cause flooring surface damage). If on snow, of course you should be standing on a relatively flat area where this will be safe to do. Place your free foot on the board, pressing close to, but in front of, the back binding. There should be that device called a stomp pad to mark this area with the purpose of giving the free foot a non skid surface. Stand balanced, pressing down on the toe side, lifting up the heel side.

Next, rock back onto your heels, lifting your toes into the air. Do these moves numerous times to help create a type of muscle memory as this will become the motion used to "apply edge" and direct control when you are actually riding the board. Try to apply torque to the board by pressing on the toes of the front foot while at the same time pushing the heel of the back foot, even though only the binding locked foot is properly able to do its job. I often begin my group clinics with these moves while indoors, out of the distractions of the mountain experience, so you should not feel foolish doing them off the slopes; however, at this point the indoor simulated (virtual) lesson must end. You are now ready for the real thing.

In a snowboard lesson the first actual movement maneuver is that of familiarizing yourself with the feeling of locomotion on the board. Check the trail traffic of a relatively flat area, and, when clear, with only the front foot buckled in, try walking across (not down) the slope. Take very small sliding movements with the free foot lined up pointing in the direction of travel in a normal body position (and the foot in the binding in that awkward knock-kneed angle). Take tiny steps with the free foot and then slide forward with the board. Step...slide. Step...slide. Warning: if you look at your feet, the desired move will not happen. Look up and things go smoothly (it's that weight/balance thing again as looking down moves weight to the rear whereas looking up reasserts the forward balance).

Cross the trail, check for traffic, and return to the original site. Depending on whether you are regular or goofy, you will have to use the board's heel or toe edge to keep it from sliding away from under you as gravity along with the waxed bottom surface both do their job, and the board keeps trying to escape and go downhill. Try this simple exercise of *skating* a second time. It is amazing to me how clumsy the first trip was and how much smoother is by the second try. You are using new muscles and movement patterns, but you will find that your body will very quickly adjust. Be sure to look up and ahead, for reasons both of balance and safety.

Unfortunately, it is exactly at this point in the lesson when guests are struggling with the clumsy weight of the board slipping out from under them that the natural reaction is to be silently asking yourself, "Why on earth have I decided to take up this sport of snowboarding?" Do not listen to that inner voice! These first minutes are the absolutely worst part of the snowboarding experience. You must remind yourself to be patient as your muscles adjust to a different stance and movement pattern. Then, all of a sudden, you will truly be enjoying yourself and having fun! I also think that these opening moments of the clinic sort of self-classify people. There no wimpy snowboarders. It takes perseverance plus stubborn determination to learn to snowboard. I am always asked if snowboarding is difficult to learn. Yes, it is, at least for these opening moments. If you want a quick-to-learn sport that takes little or no effort, then this is not the arena for you.

The Straight Glide

Next comes orienting oneself downhill. Here, terrain selection is crucial. The location on the mountain should be in a learning area with only the very slightest pitch. Many mountain guests make a serious mistake in that they assume just because a trail is marked with the green circle labeling it "easier" that it is suitable terrain for learning. This is where the expertise of your snowboard coach comes into play. The snowboard pro will know where to go away from distracting crowds and skier traffic and where the slope pitch is gentle enough for a successful learning situation. Unfortunately, many resorts lack good teaching area which in itself often leads to discouraged first timers. Do not underestimate the factor of terrain. For the experienced rider, most slopes are not of major forethought in consideration; for the beginner, simply standing upright and moving several inches downhill can be a challenge.

The *straight glide* involves placing the free back foot on the board either onto the designated stomp pad which is there to stabilize the unattached foot, or, if there is no pad, then try pushing your boot firmly against the back binding. Move forward in the flow line downhill a very short distance and ultimately dragging the toe (not the heel) of the free foot, anchor-like, to create a stop. When demonstrating the straight glide I point out my tracks in the snow showing how far the dragged toe mark goes. This is in order to emphasize the fact that it takes a long time to actually come to a stop. Learning snowboarding, as in most skill sports, requires patience and understanding. Knowing that reactions take time for their effect, it helps the beginner to know that the snowboard does not have power brakes. You will not have a sudden stop, but gradually the dragged toe will cause a ceasing of motion. I like to initially hold each person's board in place, checking out the body position to verify forward weight and eyes looking up. I ask each rider how she plans to stop, thereby confirming the fact that <u>she</u> is going to ride the board, not the board taking <u>her</u> for a ride.

As with the walking maneuver, the first attempt is usually a harrowing experience. The second try is easier. The third enactment is a "piece of cake." Although the easiest movement to instruct, this straight glide is one of the important maneuvers. Whenever going onto or off of any lift (poma, t-bar, or chairlift), the front foot is buckled in and the back foot free, and the rider must balance in this body position. To get off of a chairlift, one must do this straight glide. While practicing, it is a good idea to be sensitive kinesthetically. Experiment with hand positions and remember that in case of emergency such as descending from a difficult steep chairlift landing, placing both hands forward as if holding that imaginary tray will provide you with the most stable balanced position. Mastering the straight glide is so very basic; maintaining balance in this situation will insure a confidence level now enabling you to learn turn enactment.

The Toeside Turn

Snowboarders do not make left or right turns. Rather, these are called *heelside* or *toeside* turns, due to the fact that enactment depends upon the front foot orientation, whether regular or goofy. For the regular person, toeside brings them to the right, but it will be the opposite direction for the goofy rider. This is not a problem for the professional instructor who simply reverses the direction description and when necessary should be able to do demonstrations in both regular and goofy riding positions.

The turn is created by applying pressure on the board. If you have ever ridden a bicycle, you know that one must be in motion to create a turn. You can't jump onto the bike, quickly turn the front wheel, and expect to ride off at a sharply angled direction. Instead, the bike would shudder then fall over. It is similar on the snowboard. One must first be in motion before determining direction pressure. Therefore, start that straight glide and as soon as you feel yourself moving forward, gently begin to pressure downward with the ball of the front foot. This is an application of pressure to the toeside of the board which comes from a movement similar to that of standing on "tippie-toes." Note that it is a distinctly different move from pressing down with the toes themselves. The latter would result in "edging" which may cause you to actually tip over, falling into the turn. Instead, focus kinesthetically on pushing downward at the area where the your toes join the foot. You can exert some pressure from the back foot toes, but, because of the fact that this foot is not in the binding, it will have only a very slight effect. The board will slowly but gradually turn to the right. Nothing happens quickly. You saw how long it took to stop when toe dragging your free foot. The same slow reaction is true of the turn.   The turn will happen but not suddenly, as it is a result of gradual mounting pressure on the board edge.

It is extremely important to look in the direction of travel. You can pressure your feet until the toes crush to the bottom of the boot, but if you are frozen into a gaze straight downhill, you will go straight downhill! Look to where you wish to go.   And this bring us to the **second Golden Rule of snowboarding: WHERE YOU LOOK IS WHERE YOU**

GO! Try this toe side turn with gradual ball-of-the-foot pressure and eyes focused on your destination to the right (for regulars) or left (goofy stance) doing it at least three times until feeling confident of the move. The key to determining success is to look back at your tracks. The edge of the snowboard should leave a clear imprint of an arc cut into the snow.

The Heelside Turn

I have always found the word "heelside" to be problematic. The name of this turn is confusing in that it refers to the board's anatomy, not the rider's. What I mean is, yes, the direction is oriented on the heel side of the board, but the turn is caused by pressure **on the ankle area, not the heel** of the rider. Since the body motion is always forward, then the pushing forward onto the heel side necessitates pressuring on the outside ankle of that front foot. For example, if a rider with regular, not goofy stance, it would require pressure on the left ankle of the left foot; goofy stance would call for pressuring the right ankle of the right foot. If instead, the rider rocks back onto her heels, the weight goes back (you don't want that!) and she will fall over backwards.

A disturbing aspect of the heelside turn is involved in creating the stop. One steps off with the free foot to enact that anchor-drag, but the movement is in the opposite direction of the turn due to the fact that you are standing oriented sideways on the snowboard. A regular stance person would have been heading left, but the stepping off foot abruptly pulls her to the right; goofy stance step off aborts the right direction of travel with a sudden shift to the left. Beware! It is very easy to pull a muscle in the upper inside part of the thigh. Therefore, the turn should be done very slowly and not ridden out a far distance, otherwise there is that inherent risk of picking up speed and the subsequent muscle injury.

The process of instruction is the same as that for the toeside turn. One begins with a controlled straight glide, then gently pressuring that forward part of the ankle and looking in the desired direction of travel. These factors will cause the desired turn which, for regulars, will go to the left and for the goofies, to the right. Practice makes perfect, and again, a trio of turns will give adequate experience.

My group clinics of about eight guests usually require a full hour to reach this point of instruction. It is always fascinating to see that by now these beginners will have mastered walking around which initially was so challenging but now requires no thought or special effort at all. The straight glide is a confidence builder, and those who had found the toeside turn to be difficult usually have an easy time with the heelside, and the opposite is true for others. Ironically, the situation tends to reverse itself. Masters of the toeside suddenly become efficient at heelside, but at a loss of the former. It sort of comes and goes, but fortunately, eventually all evens out once both feet are firmly in the bindings which is exactly what comes next.

7

The Moment of Truth:

Both Feet Buckled In

This is a reminder that the first five chapters have only focused on preparation for the snowboarding experience. From Chapter 6 forward, I have tried to anticipate and explain the typical lesson and moves to be mastered. As stated earlier, this is not a do-it-yourself-guide. Instead, hopefully, after spending lesson time with a certified instructor, you will study these pages and further understand what you were attempting or have duly accomplished out there on the hill.

The Responsibility Code

A good start is awareness of the Mountain Experience Responsibility Code. These rules are often posted at ski areas and are mentioned by instructors, but they are certainly important enough to be relevant and deserving of your full attention at this moment.

1. Snowboard in control.
     This means that you must have the ability to stop or turn in order to avoid running into people or objects.

Snowboarding for Women

2. If you overtake another skier/snowboarder, <u>you</u> have the responsibility of avoiding them.
   If you are coming downhill, you must not run into the person ahead of you. This includes when doing jumps or coming suddenly onto a trail from in the woods.

3. Do not stop and block the trail.
   Unlike the skier who can stop and balance standing without moving, when Betty Shred snowboarder stops, she cannot balance, and therefore must sit down. Be sure that you are sitting on the side of the trail and not blocking it or not out of view in a place where oncoming skiers and riders cannot see you.

4. Before entering a trail or traversing, look uphill and yield to those coming.

5. Observe closed trail signs and ropes.
   Closed trails are posted as such for your safety. Every season there are snowboarders who die when they fall into tree wells. The soft snow in the woods may look attractive, but it is easy to lose balance on ungroomed terrain where there are hidden stumps and other debris close under the snow surface.   Ski patrol does not "sweep" these off limits areas, so you are on your own in terms of seeking rescue if lost.

6. You should have a safety strap (leash) on your board.
   Remember to hold onto your leash when first buckling in, as boards tend to take off rather quickly on their own.

7. Know how to use the lifts.

If you are not familiar with how to ride the lift, ask the operator for help.

These rules appear to deal with etiquette, but they also relate to safety. If you ride out of control, you not only put yourself at risk, but also endanger the safety of others. It's been such a long struggle over the years for snowboarding acceptance at ski areas, so it is incumbent upon us to be extra responsible and be good snowsport citizens.

Now that you know the rules, how does one actually *do* it?

The Moment of Truth

This is the moment you have planned for, shopped for, outfitted for, traveled for, and signed up for! Remembering the fact that you are standing on a slippery surface, one does not want to take off downhill so be sure that you are standing with your board directed across the trail, rather than as if you were to start riding straight down the slope. Now sit down. You should be sitting on the snow, facing down the hill and now buckling in both feet. **Do not stand up!**

Although it seems scary, with the back foot buckled in you will actually have much more ability to balance and properly control the board than before. Two feet buckled means twice the pressure power as before. The initial instructional stage of one foot off the board was not really a true sampling of what it is like to snowboard, because it only suggested a situation which is rarely enacted in terms of the time you spend on snow. Getting on or off a lift is momentary; the rest of the lesson time you are on the board with both feet

101

buckled in. At this juncture there will be introduced new movements involving *edging (tilting)* and *twisting (applying torque* to) the board. For the best vantage starting point, the regular rider will be to the left side of the trail when facing down hill; the goofy should be on the opposite right side. This results in being toeside, the easiest way to start, when doing the initial *traverse* (movement across the trail).

The first thing is to understand is mobility. You are not like a turtle on its back. Instead, you have quite a range of movement. This is a good time to understand and accept the fact that snowboarders spend a lot of time sitting around on the snow, so you had might as well get used to it. Lay down as if you were making snow angels. When was the last time you rolled in the snow? This is part of the fun (and a reminder of how much of life we lose as we become such serious adults).

If you are a regular, stretch your right arm outward, lift your legs (with board attached), and roll over towards your right side onto your stomach. If you are goofy, stretch out your left arm to brace yourself as you roll over in that direction. You most likely will be laughing at these gymnastics, but without learning how to roll over, you will be sort of "beached" upon the snow. You should now be facing uphill and on your knees. Without standing upright, you can shift-slide left or right. You can also do a frog leap forward up the hill. You will soon find yourself doing all of these moves at various times on the mountain.

Rolling over to face uphill is a good habit to form because once you get onto steeper terrain you will find it relatively impossible to stand up facing downhill. I remember a conversation I once had with a young woman in the ski lodge cafeteria during lunch. She had spent the morning learning to snowboard, and, in response to my question of how she felt, she complained bitterly about her aching wrists. Of course, I made my usual little speech about never reaching out with your arm to break a fall as the pressure is simply too much for the wrist to absorb. "Oh, no," she said. "My wrists hurt from pushing myself up each time I fall." Thus, I learned of still another reason to roll over and get up facing uphill. However, the most important reason to do so is that facing uphill before resuming an upright position allows you to see if there is oncoming skier/snowboarder traffic. Don't initiate riding until the coast is clear.

One note: adolescent girls often find it difficult to do that rolling over move. This is due to a lack of development of stomach muscles. A friend nearby can help them to swing over their legs or they can grasp the back of the thigh to help guide the movement. Women who have difficulty will be reminded to do some sit-up exercises when they return home from vacation. They will not only become more agile snowboarders, but also will have the bonus of a flatter stomach, something we all yearn for.

Ready to stand up? First, know that there is a movement called edging. Remember when you first put on the snowboard and leaned on its edges to make marks in the snow? Those edges of the board are sharp and they are your brakes since you no longer have a free foot to drag in order to stop. As you slowly rise finding balance, use that uphill edge to hold you. Dig it into the snow. Too much edge, you will fall down onto your knees; too little, you will flop back downhill. Find the amount of edging which works for you.

At this point in a lesson, as the instructor, I am never further than several <u>inches</u> (!) away and my hands are either holding onto the person or ready to do so. Remember that practice of the toeside glide from Chapter 6 where pressure on the ball of the foot causes the board to turn to the toeside direction (for the regular rider, this is a right turn). You do not want to go straight down the hill; rather, the desired direction of travel is to go from the left side of the trail across the hill to the right side in a traverse. Now you will apply the newly added skill of edging. Pressure and vision create direction; edging gives control. Keeping your eyes focused upon your destination <u>across</u> the trail, allow the board to slowly glide by releasing the edge just enough to let it move while gently asserting pressure on the ball of the foot. Be ready to tilt the board onto its edge if you feel the movement is too fast for your comfort zone.

Edging

Be assertive! Do not let that board take you for a ride! You have the ability to control all movement. If vision is an element in this control, then use it wisely. If where you look is where you go, then why not look uphill? You can't ride uphill, so simply looking in that direction will naturally slow you down. Then, at the same time, press hard on that uphill edge of the board. Dig it in so hard that the board will cut the snow as you rock forward onto the toeside edge. Press down really hard with both feet to tilt the board. Those are your brakes! The first time, like a new driver who slams on the brakes too hard, you will rock forward with a sudden stop. Reassert your balance. Now reapply pressure to resume movement across the hill. Keep testing those brakes gently, and you will quickly get the hang of it. Suddenly, sooner than you would ever expect, you will feel the thrill of actually riding the snowboard.

Chapter 7 The Moment of Truth

A note of safety in terms of your own self. One seldom learns to snowboard without ever falling. The trick is to understand and accept this fact and allow the fall to happen. Injuries occur (usually to the wrist or shoulder) when the rider reaches out to use an arm or hand to break a fall. As already stated, the wrist is a very small and vulnerable joint, especially if it is called upon to brace your entire body weight. When you think that you will lose balance, simply sit down. If you feel that you are falling forward, then drop to your knees (see Chapter 3 on wearing knee pads).

Arms should be kept close to the body and never extended to prevent a fall. Falling does not have to mean being open to injury; it's just something which is part of the territory, although I truly believe that it is possible to give a no-falls lesson. Slow careful movements with patience in learning along with wise selection of terrain and good snow conditions are all important factors in a safe learning situation. Women tend to do well with such specifically choreographed steps. They never seem to try to muscle their way across the hill but are good at these refined and more subtle body moves.

Using those specific skills of pressure, vision (where you look, whether across or up the hill) and tilting, one traverses the trail, comes to a total stop by jamming the toeside (for regular riders) edge super hard into the snow surface, and gently falling to (padded) knees. Be sure to look back. It is important to see accomplishment. You should mentally congratulate yourself on the distance you have traveled, all done with control of the board. Note the tracks you have left behind, and you will see where each time you forcefully edged to slow down and brake the speed of forward movement. Good job.

Snowboarding for Women

Ready to go the other way? Slowly stand, and, believe it or not, because this is much easier to do than it sounds, you will simply jump in the air and turn yourself around. Not all the way in a circle but just 90°, part way around, so that you will be in the same posture facing straight downhill as when we were learning to do the straight glide. It helps to have a coach who steadies your board at this moment. You will now enact a heelside turn.

Looking across the hill, the heelside edge is now the uphill edge of the board. Some find this frightening because they tend to look straight down the hill, so it is important to focus on the direction of travel which is across. It should be of some comfort to know that this heelside body position is actually the stronger posture compared to toeside . If you want to crush a soda can, would you do it with your heel or your toe? Certainly, with the heel. This is because your heel side uses skeletal strength, whereas the toe uses muscle. You should feel confident as you slow down (with edging) by rocking gently onto your heels and tilting the board, which acts as your method of braking as you slide forward and then edge again.

Move forward, then edge. Move forward, then edge. Control that board! With confidence of control you already should be having a good time out there! To stop, give an extra sharp jab with the heels down into the snow (skiers are usually good at this move as it is similar to the hockey stop), and then drop down into a sitting position. Rest, relax, and be proud of yourself. Look back at the trail to see your movement tracks, look up at the sky and appreciate the weather, look at the other folks out on the trail and be happy to be there with them and doing your own thing!

Each time you have finished going heelside you should

come to a full stop; sit down and roll over. Continue practicing these traverses across the hill until you are really feeling in control of your moves. At first you may feel as if you are flying, but gradually you will get the knack for the proper amount of edging needed to control your speed. Note that your pattern of travel has been across, not down, the trail. Snowboarding is neither like sledding with its motion directly down what we call the *flow* or *fall line* (akin to the path a snowball would take to roll down a hill), nor does snowboarding always follow the skier's direction of travel down the mountain. Geometry has taught us that the shortest distance between two points is a straight line, but the snowboarder disregards this mathematical axiom. The fun is in the riding of the board rather than at reaching the final destination. That is why one sees skiers, although turning, usually observed to be in a very big hurry to get to the bottom of the trail, whereas the snowboarders are meandering down, often stopping to ride a little snowbank on the sides. Their mind set is different from that of the skier and another reason why the sport seems to appeal to women. Absent is the competitive race down the mountain. There is plenty of time to enjoy the scenery along the way.

Linking Turns: As Easy As 1-2-3

It is usually when attempting to *link turns* (which means coming down the slope, turning without stopping) that people tend to experience what is called "the snowboarder's slam." Don't let it happen to you! There is a very simple way to avoid such a crash which is caused by catching the downhill edge. Using a 1-2-3 principle, know that there are three steps to linking a turn.

#1 You have done your traverse on, let us say, your toeside
    edge. Come almost, but not completely, to a stop.
#2 Looking downhill, steering with your feet, allow the board
    to go completely flat. This is a scary moment because
    the board takes off directly down the mountain. Count
    quickly, "1-2-3" which should actually take less than
    three seconds.
#3 Look across the slope and (leading with your ankle) ride
onto the heelside of the board.

The reason people tend to crash while attempting to link
turns is because the snowboard will not allow you to switch
from one edge directly onto the other edge. The board must
have a middle sequence wherein it has no edging at all. Think
of it as a shift car in that you must push in the clutch to change
gears. You must go to neutral in order to change direction.
Allowing the board to be flat, even for the slightest instant,
permits you to change edge pressure and direction of travel.
It's really as easy as 1-2-3.

The Pivot

In case you didn't notice the phrase, I mentioned
"steering with your feet" as the way to turn the board in the
process of making a turn. What this really involves is moving
the board into the desired direction of travel. Years ago, when
the design of snowboards was much more primitive, instructors
would teach people to reach out twisting the upper body and
pointing with their arms to create a turn. Nowadays
snowboards are products of sophisticated engineering and
upper body rotation is not only unnecessary in this situation but
also undesirable. To turn the board with minimum effort and
ride with flow, one simply moves both legs to pivot the board.

Chapter 7 The Moment of Truth

This is what is meant by foot steering as it is an active movement of both feet to direct the board. Remember that snowboarding happens because of crucial movements from the foot to the knee. That's the region where everything is happening. We all have a goal of looking good, and looking good is predicated upon a quiet upper body as you seem to glide effortlessly down the trail.

You should now go into the ski lodge to take a well deserved rest.

NO

YES

8
Take a Break

Hydration

Wanting to take a break is often a polite euphemism for stating the need to find time to go to the ladies' room. I know that this is a weird sounding suggestion, but be sure that you remember before flushing the toilet to look at the color of your urine. The brighter the yellow color, the more evidence you will have of your condition of dehydration. Nowadays we tend to be quite aware of the need to drink plenty of water. It's almost considered fashionable by some women to walk around carrying a water bottle. Unfortunately, one does not usually consider the need to hydrate when doing a winter sport. Snowboarding is a dynamic sport and, as you have seen, requires a great deal of body movement. With excessive body movement comes perspiration which, thanks to the wicking quality of your undergarments, will not have you feeling sweaty; but, nevertheless, there will be the need to replenish those lost body fluids. Also, if you have been out partying last night, chances are that you have arrived at the mountain rather dehydrated before you even buckled into your snowboard bindings.

The truth is that there is actually a greater danger from the effects of dehydration in the winter time than in summer, mostly because you would never suspect it. Dehydration leads

111

to a situation where the body has difficulty regulating its own temperature, and this can actually result in frostbite or even hypothermia. To add to the problem, people often think that they are hungry when, in reality, they are thirsty. By the time you are thirsty, the body is already in serious need of fluids. So--while you are taking a break this is an optimum time to refuel the body with liquids. You have been concentrating hard and doing an athletic activity. Even if you don't feel thirsty or even sweaty, treat yourself to a good drink. But, of what?

To compound the problem of dehydration is the fact that the traditional beverage drink when entering a ski lodge is hot chocolate, which contains caffeine, a mild diuretic, thus only increasing rather than decreasing your state of dehydration. Sugar slows down the body's ability to absorb fluids, therefore eliminating the desirability in this circumstance of soft drinks whose only true benefit is in their ice cubes. Coffee is certainly in the same category with hot chocolate in its caffeine content. What's left? Decaf tea, decaf coffee, sport drinks, and good oldfashioned water. Not only will you feel more comfortable out there on the hill after a water break, but hydration leads to better mental concentration and physical coordination, plus, if in high altitude, it definitely tends to ward off altitude sickness symptoms.

Frostbite

Since I have just mentioned the two conditions of frostbite and hypothermia, it is probably a good idea to give some specifics. Frostbite occurs when the skin freezes. This is a real hazard on very cold days with low temperatures, exacerbated with wind (the wind chill factor). The best defense against frostbite is covering exposed skin with a neck gaiter or face mask and a generous application of a frost guard cream (see Chapter 2). The best safeguard is to simply accept the fact that you are cold and go inside. But people, particularly in a group situation, do not like to be the first to say that they are cold. When one person meekly suggests that she is freezing, only then do others in the group tend to agree to take a break although usually with a confidential whisper that they are also totally chilled.

Years ago I was giving a private snowboarding lesson on a very cold day. Although I was wearing soft boots, my feet were really chilled, and I wanted to go into the lodge for a warm-up break. My client was wearing hard boots so her feet must have been considerably colder than mine were, but she insisted that she was just fine. I didn't press the point because, after all, she was paying a steep price for that private lesson, and I presumed that she didn't want to waste her money on hearing me talk about instruction while indoors. Finally, I was so cold that I insisted we take a short break. When we went inside she then realized that her feet were so numb that there was no more feeling in her toes. We finished the lesson there in the cafeteria.

Some time later I received a letter of thanks from this woman. She had developed frostbite on her toes, and her doctor said that coming inside when we did certainly saved her from a very severe case. Now that I am more experienced, I am more insistent. If I am cold, since I always seem to be dressed warmer than anyone else, then it must really be cold, and, since I am the instructor and therefore in charge of the situation, we all go in!

What does frostbite look like? Do you know the fuzzy white frost which develops on the outside of frozen juice cans?

That's just what it looks like on a person's skin. A patch forms, often ranging from the size of a dime to that of a quarter, where the skin first turns very white and then frost will appear. Treatment is simple. Watch for the appearance of a white area and then, <u>without rubbing</u>, place a non-mittened finger on the spot. The warmth of skin against the skin of the frostbite area will do the trick. Then, go indoors out of the cold! Remember in my discussion of jewelry that metal conducts temperature (women who cook know that when you make instant soup, you never put hot water into the can without holding it with a potholder or it will be too hot to hold). Applying that principle, if you are wearing earrings it means that your ear lobes will be more susceptible to frostbite; nose rings, eyebrow rings, etc. have obviously similar risks. I watch my students' complexions closely, particularly those with such abovementioned body piercing, and I request that they do the same for me.

Hypothermia

Hypothermia occurs when a person becomes so very cold that the body temperature drops. Symptoms are fatigue, difficulty concentrating, lack of coordination, and most noticeably, shivering. It's easy to be aware of this danger when there are sub-zero conditions, but people can succumb to hypothermia in more moderate temperatures when it is misting or raining. Dampness takes away body heat, particularly when accompanied by windy conditions. Thus, unexpected cases of hypothermia can occur in weather temperatures which range from 32 to even 50 degrees, given the situation of rapid heat loss due to wind and rain. Safeguard: just be sure that you are dressed a little bit warmer than you would normally be in situations when you will be exposed to prolonged dampness.

With so many hazards, why get involved at all in this crazy sport?

On the contrary, it is simply more proof that snowboarding is so much fun that we do it in spite of the negative situations and risks involved. Why else would one drive for hours in bad weather on snowy roads, pay resort prices for hotel accommodations, worry about strategically dressing for varying temperatures, and go through complicated arrangements for equipment and instruction? It's a sport which will pay you back many times over in pleasure for the inconvenience involved and energy expended.

9

Reverse Gravity:
What Comes Down Must Go Up

Before you even think about *how* to ride a lift, first decide *where* you want to go. That may sound obvious, but so many times people wind up on the wrong trails simply because of failure to study the resort map. When finishing a clinic, ask your instructor for advice on what trails would be appropriate for your ability level. The green circle emblem designates easier trails, the blue square marks more difficult trails, the black diamond is for most difficult and the orange lozenge announces the terrain park. There are no plus or minus signs within the three categories which means that some of these trails may be relatively easy for their labeling, while others are much more challenging. Also, snow conditions are a major factor. Ice can make that easier green trail into a black most difficult one. Conversely, fresh powder is what we call "ego snow" because it slows everything down and is forgiving of your mistakes and can make difficult trails into a pleasure ride. Even the time of day has an influence, not only because of the weather's impact upon the surface in terms of softening up or freezing, but because as the day goes on, the trail surface may become slick and slippery with an appreciable depth of snow scraped off from the skier traffic. The smoothly groomed trail of 9:00 a.m. may be a serious mogul (bump) field by 3:00 p.m. Ask around before selecting a lift; choose your destination wisely. This is simply another example of an assertive attitude. It may seem carefree to randomly go where the closest lift takes you, but you might not be so happy once faced with the prospect of coming down the trails serviced by that lift.

The introduction to this book mentions the subject of chairlifts and the fact that many women, generally speaking, tend to be rather terrified at the prospect of riding a chairlift, much less with a snowboard awkwardly dangling from their feet. One gets over this inhibition when faced with the prospect of hiking or mastering one of the non-airborne types of lifts which pull you uphill as you must balance on the snow. We know that according to the laws of physics, what goes up must come down. As a snowboarder, however, I am more concerned with the fact that to go down, one must go up.

For all lifts, except gondolas and trams where you carry your equipment inside, your front foot is buckled in, the back foot left free. Now is the time to review your skating and the straight glide, both of which were usually the first maneuvers you did when learning to snowboard. This is especially important if it is the first time you are out for the season or if time has elapsed since you have been riding. Go to an area which is not congested and review these motions of walking and sliding the board forward with the free back foot on the stomp pad. Then you will be ready to enter the lift maze.

The easiest of the surface lifts, or "drags" as they are called in Europe, is the *poma*, a disc suspended on a spring. I like to ride the poma with the disk under my right arm (under

118

the left arm for goofy riders), tucked up tight above the elbow towards the armpit so it will not pop out. Balance with free foot on the stomp pad, leaning back slightly to compensate for the initial forward jolt and ready to then transfer weight onto the front foot. Hold the post with both hands, look ahead at the tracks, and enjoy the ride. Getting off is easy. Just let the disc slip out, and it will pull up out of your way.

If the poma runs for a very long distance, as is the case in some European ski areas, then it is better to place the disc between your legs up near the crotch. Do not sit down, and do not let it pop out. Of course, such advice is easier said than done. Skiers place the poma disc between their legs, but it is easier for them as they face frontward, not in the snowboarder's sideways stance. The worst poma I ever went on was in Italy. The lift traveled up along a ridge with a horrendous drop on one side. Fear of falling off was what made me stay on! Another unforgettable poma was in Chile where, after a long steep haul, it then made a 90 degree turn and continued onward and upward. In comparison, pomas in the United States are quite user friendly.

On the other hand, the worst *t-bar* I ever went on was at that same Chilean resort, mostly because it just seemed endless. The t-bar is a hook shaped wooden bar which is placed behind your rear, as if it were a seat, but you cannot sit on it. The trick is to balance enough on the bar as it pulls you uphill without allowing it to slip out from under you. As with the poma, you look at the path, balance on the front foot, and really focus on maintaining this precarious position. The good news for both of these lift systems is that if you do fall off, (usually) there is no fearful drop because you were on the ground surface all the time.

Snowboarding for Women

Compared to the prospect of managing to balance on these surface lifts, even a person who is afraid of heights realizes that the chair lift is starting to look like an appealing alternative. In fact, once you have succeeded in getting onto the chair seat, it's rather comfy. As with other lifts, the front foot is buckled in; the back foot is out. For your very first attempt it is best to ride on a lift with someone experienced, but not on a full chair. In other words, if it is a "quad" which seats four, request to ride as a threesome. This will give you more maneuverability room when getting off at the end. You can also signal the operator at the top that you would like the chair slowed down to make it easier to disembark.

Move up to what is usually a marked line for the loading zone, look over your shoulder to see the chair coming towards you, sit when you feel it bump the back of your legs, pull down the safety bar (warning your lift companions so that their hands or heads are not at risk), and enjoy the ride. If you are nervous or feel queasy about the height, simply do not look down. For those who find the weight of a dangling board uncomfortable, one can balance the board somewhat horizontally over the toe box area of your free foot which then acts as a support under it.

While riding the chair is a good time to watch and study other riders beneath you. Do some mental coaching in observing their strong moves which will help you in creating an image of how *you* will be handling the same trail. Some useful "don't's" for the chair ride: don't fuss with your hat because you may drop it; don't ever take off a glove because you will be sure to drop it! Instead, talk to your lift companions who may be as nervous as you are. Pay attention to the length of the ride in order to be ready to unload in time.

Chapter 9 Reverse Gravity

I advise my students on a foolproof way to dechair. First, plan ahead by placing your free foot on the stomp pad. Look down at this placement. Relax and feel free to move that foot away. You will NOT glance there again, but, trust me, you will remember upon landing where to put your back foot onto the board. As you approach the landing area the chair may slow down if it is a "detachable." First steady yourself with hands on the edge of the chair seat, and don't worry. Now, as the chair reaches the unloading area, be ready to stand, weight on the front foot, free foot on that stomp pad, looking ahead to where you want to go.

The secret ingredient is that you should hold both arms straight out in front of you while looking up, not down. Direct your vision forward using your arms as a sight line. Don't be concerned; because you had simulated the move, that back foot will find its place on the stomp pad. Note that if, instead, the free foot is set on the snow, one tends to spin around it (similar to the way the fixed point of a draftsman's compass needle causes the pencil to circle). The outreaching arm position will bring your weight forward and initiate the motion needed to glide off. You may look silly with this arms out position, but you will look sillier if you do not do that and instead look downwards or place your free foot on snow, both guaranteed to make you fall!

You will soon realize that the biggest problem in getting off the chairlift concerns the skiers who are stopped in the unloading zone. They carry their poles in hand for the chair ride and now are busy affixing the strap handles over bulky mittens or gloves, totally unaware of their blocking the chair exit area. Mountain courtesy and safety both encourage you to yell ahead: "Excuse me, please clear the way!" It is a much

Snowboarding for Women

better strategy than crashing into them.

Be sure to move quickly out of the path of the chairlift and go out of the way because you will now have to sit down, buckle up, and orient yourself as to your destination.

And on to the next Thing

10

Is That All I Need to Know?

By now, you are rather proficient at doing both a heelside and toeside traverse (in non-snowboarding language: going either direction diagonally across the trail), and your ability to link turns is actually getting impressive. Now you feel ready to do it all.

Continuing Education

A problem is that at this point people tend to think that their instructional learning phase is done. Wrong. Although the resort area's special introduction to snowboarding program might have ended, it doesn't mean that you are *there* in terms of learning and accomplishment. Snowboarding consists of more than basic traverses on extremely moderate terrain. On the other hand, this does not mean that you must take costly private lessons. Check the resort's marketing brochure for the clinic programs which are usually quite a bargain because the industry is geared to keeping people interested once they have become engaged in a snowsport. An advantage of the clinic is that friendships are formed within the group so that often you will have companions for free riding when the clinic ends. If

125

you can afford it, private lessons offer the luxury of instruction geared to your own rate of progress plus the potential for a continued relationship with one snowboarding pro as your coach. Either way, it beats going out on your own trying to remember what the instructor told you last week, or what you *think* you were told. Memory is deceptive with the added factor that differing snow conditions require different techniques.

The "You Can Do It" Syndrome

Beware of overconfidence and beware of friends who invite you to come along to ride difficult trails with them, reassuring you with the words, "You can do it." Human nature is such that once people have learned to do certain skills, they tend to forget or discount their own initial fears and difficulties. They have already forgotten what it was like for them as a beginner and easily underestimate the difficulty which confronts you. You will survive, but at a cost in terms of doing a lot of falling down and generally bashing your body. Falling is a very negative thing. It is not only demoralizing, but it can cause injury. Yes, one learns with challenge, but being brought onto too difficult terrain and being discouraged is not exactly productive. Gaining mileage is key to improvement, but terrain selection is a critical element. Also, supervised moves with a qualified instructor are the way to go. It's a situation of quantity plus quality

The Falling Leaf

I always am reminded of an E.E. Cummings poem when teaching the falling leaf because, although the poet's theme is

126

the subject of loneliness, the letters inside his parentheses conjure up the solitary image of the back and forth swaying floating motion of a single leaf as it falls from the tree to the ground:

l(a

le
af
fa

ll

s)
one
l

iness

from *E.E.Cummings: Complete Poems 1904-1962,* edited by George J. Firmage, Liveright, New York, 1991, p. 673.

You can recall the image of this poem because the letters enclosed in the parentheses spell out "a leaf falls" and create the same image as the motion you are enacting on your snowboard. The falling leaf snowboard action is basically a pendulum-like movement to the right and to the left progressing downhill on the trail.

This action is easiest to begin learning to do from the heelside position. You are standing on the board, facing downhill. Remember that where you look causes direction, and pressure on the front of the board creates the desired force. Now, turning your head to look over your left shoulder, add the weight of both arms by swinging them over to the same side. You will move horizontally on a slight diagonal across the hill. Just go several feet, then rock back onto your heels (tilting the board to enact edging) to stop. Next, look the opposite way to the right. Swing your arms onto that direction, and weight your back foot, which will cause you to slide backwards. Then tilt the board on edge again to stop. Yes, the back foot. You will have gone in reverse horizontally on the diagonal, near where you started, but considerably lower down on the slope.

This is possibly the most important maneuver you will ever learn for survival on terrain which is too difficult for you to ride. Do the falling leaf, sliding from side to side, going forwards and then riding backwards, a number of times. Turn around and see how far downhill you have efficiently traveled. This is the technique to use when the slope is too steep, you are too frightened to turn, and/or you are afraid for whatever reason to come down any portion of a trail. Once learned, it is easy to do, and it will literally save you. Practice on the toeside, but know that this will quickly become tiring because the calves of your legs will get quite a workout. Remember that toeside relies upon muscles, whereas heelside uses the body skeleton for pressure support. That is why the heelside falling leaf is a thing to practice until it has become an integral part of your riding repertoire.

Riding Switch

You've already done this freestyle maneuver. When you went backwards doing the falling leaf you were riding *fakie*. That was simply going backwards in a traverse. Riding backwards with linked turns is referred to in snowboard jargon as *riding switch*. This is a fun thing to do and is a requisite introduction to free style tricks. It's also handy when you are in a jam and don't have the room or maneuverability to go forward. Think of your intro lesson to riding: pressure on the front foot, looking in that direction. Just do the exact opposite: pressure on the back foot, twisting around your upper body to look in that backward direction. You are doing a reverse of the norm, having switched. What was the nose of the board is now, in effect, its tail. Concentrate on how you previously have made a forward turn with head and shoulders aligned. Do it in the reverse direction.

If it feels awkward, that is an expected reaction because your lower body will be twisted since your feet are set in what was originally a forward facing angled binding, now oriented backwards. Those who do a lot of switch riding tend to have a *duck feet* binding setting (each foot with heels together, toes pointing outward in opposite direction, ballet style) and use a free-style (twin tip) board which is designed for movement in either direction. To help you feel more balanced, try working your knees pointing inward when toeside and outward, cowboy style, when heelside, causing the board to flex torsionally.   Do a fakie traverse, allowing the board to seek the fall line, then be sure to lean downhill with bent flexed knees oriented as stated above, looking across to enter the new traverse and finish the turn. Be sure that your practice is done on a very flat learning area.

The Straight Slide

The straight slide is another emergency technique to use when you want to get down an area of the trail without doing a traverse or trying to turn, although it is not as sophisticated a move as the falling leaf and, therefore, not really as effective.

One simply tilts the board onto its uphill edge and allows it to slide slightly, controlling the speed of the gravity-pull acceleration with reassertion of the pressure tilt which puts the board on edge as a way of applying the brakes. The maneuver works, but your body may feel like a jackhammer as you rumble over the surface for a prolonged period of time.

Garlands

As you must have observed, imagery is very important in snowboard coaching, and the garland reminds one of the Christmas tree decorations which drape from branch to branch. You will trace these loops on the snow in a modified traverse. Instead of going diagonally across the trail, go about one third of the way and then head uphill (look uphill and pressure the front foot). You can't ride uphill, so the board will then proceed to slide backwards. Allow it to do so for a few feet, sort of rocking backwards. Tilt the board on edge to stop, and then, reasserting your direction, go another third of the way across the hill, repeating the uphill motion. Rock back, then go to the final segment of the trail. The good thing about doing garlands is that you get many chances to control the board as it traverses, rather than going all the way across the trail, cutting through downhill traffic, and then worrying about what will happen when you eventually reach the other side. Doing garlands is a wonderful technique for confidence building because you are riding the board, not letting the board take you for a ride. Picture in your mind those Christmas tree garlands and sing *Jingle Bells* as you go! That's not really facetious; the image will help plus the fact that singing not only relaxes you, but it also helps create rhythmic moves.

Looking Good with Shapely Turns

Looking good on the snowboard results from feeling at ease. The more confident you are, the better you will look. One way to help achieve rhythm is to understand turn shape. The goal is to make round turns. To pivot is to rotate about an axis. Although the pivot is really an important move, particularly when faced with uneven bumped up surfaces (these are called *moguls*), it is often a problem when novice riders indiscriminately pivot their turns. Pivoted turns spin around to change direction. They are quick which is why the rider employs them because the time facing the fall line is frightening, and we want it to be only for the briefest instant; however, the effect is jagged, and the resultant move is what I call windshield wiper turns.

With confidence comes trust in your ability to slow down and negotiate the turn with slow soft pressure and wide arcing moves. Think of the turn as having three distinct regions: the beginning, middle, and the end. The first phase is easy, but the middle finds you facing directly downhill which is scary. It is here that one must calmly and gently direct the board using foot steering and a twist of pressure to create torque. Sorry for the technical terms, but pressure on the front with slightly lesser pressure done by the back foot on the opposite rear edge will cause the board to employ what is called *torsional flex*. It will glide smoothly through the turn. I tell my students that it's all basically reduced to a Kierkegaardian leap of faith; you have to believe in it, and then it will happen. Too much back foot pressure causes abrupt turns, which we refer to as "hitch-kicking," so this will take some careful consideration to get the right refinement of timing and pressure. Rather than focusing on the physics involved, simply try to round out the turns into giant curved C shapes.

Actually, it's sort of fun to experiment with turn shapes in regard to the alphabet. Do some Z shaped turns to help define your goal of a C shaped turn. How about trying an S turn, or even a J turn? The former simply means that the turns are a C shape followed by a C done reversed, but the latter J is an exciting challenge as one goes straight downhill then is "saved" by a rounded turn out of the fall line. Try J and reverse J turns (always reverting to easier terrain when experimenting with new moves), and you will really gain confidence in your turning ability. Skiers call these *fish hook turns* because at the end there is a backwards slide (similar to that which occurs when doing garlands).

By now you must realize that you are no longer in the beginner category, and you will have loosened up on the axiom of weight on the front foot. Back foot pressure is needed to do the falling leaf, the garlands, and the J turns. In truth, if we had x-ray eyes to see into the boot, we would notice that the crucial joint at work here is the ankle which flexes so that pressure moves are initiated from the toe or heel of the foot, and within those areas we can see that the pressure is moving from the big toe across the foot to the little toe, all during the turn sequence. Your back foot is starting to play a more active role. Relax, and your body will work out the best way for you to balance with sensitivity to adjust stance not only fore to aft on the board but also vertically by flexing the knees.

Another variation on the turn has to do with frequency. One can make big fat long turns which swallow up much of the trail. These are called *wide radius turns* and tend to be good practice as one has plenty of time to ride the edge of the board and concentrate on the roundness of the turn shape. Steeper terrain calls for *short radius turns*. These are done quicker and take up less space as they are done more in the fall line. Imagine that the trail you are on is only of limited width and that you have no choice but to keep turning. How many turns in a row can you make? Try doing a spiral, starting with wide radius turns and then reducing their size until they are narrower and narrower. Next, do a reverse spiral, with turns getting larger and larger. Look ahead to a specified point such as a tree alongside the trail or a lift tower, and see how many turns it will take for you to arrive at the destination. There is use for all size turns. It is a good idea to know that you can and should be varying your turns without compromising the desired round shape. One caution, however, is to make these balanced as we all have a tendency to favor one direction and thus hold the turn longer when going that way.

More Games

Another fun thing to do with turns is experimenting with arm/hand position. Try making a turn with your hands in different positions: *ie*. on top of your head, hanging down at your sides, raised in front as if holding a tray, clasped behind your back, akimbo at the hips, or straight out like airplane wings. You will quickly find out how your turns are initiated. The turn should be enacted with movement originating from the foot to the knee. The upper body should be quiet. If you are off balance on your turns, do these above mentioned hand position drills repeatedly to get rid of upper body movement (we call that *rotation*), and instead you will learn to glide through with a balanced smoothness. I once spent an entire season working on riding with my hands behind my back, Hans Brinker style. It was fun and helped me to focus on my balancing along with eliminating wasted upper body motion.

The airplane wings image may be used in another drill which is also done instead by some snowboard instructors with the use of bamboo poles. When traversing the hill, your body should be perpendicular (remember your geometry), which results with shoulders being parallel to the slope of the trail surface. In effect, because the hill slopes, you should also slope. In other words, your uphill shoulder should be higher than your downhill shoulder. When you turn to traverse to the opposite direction, the shoulder positioning should also be reversed. Try that airplane wing arm posture, and you will quickly see the obvious. Do it with a partner and report to each other on your observations. This is the same principle which runners use as they lean forward downward when running downhill instead of pulling back which is counterproductive. The lower downhill shoulder will help you create a smoother more balanced turn.

Bend Ze Knees, Five Dollars Pleeze

The above phrase was always the classic ski instructors' joke. Learning to ski was reduced to a matter of bending the knees. Snowboarders must also bend their knees, but it is interesting to self experiment to fully understand the effect. Do a traverse across and back, riding the board as low as you can possibly go. Next, start low then suddenly stand very tall, as if someone were pulling you erect, caveman style, by the hair. How did it feel? Which way had you going faster? Slower? Staying low on the board exerts pressure which slows you down. The sudden rise results in what we call *unweighting* and the board will pick up speed. Do not take my word for it as it is important that you can feel the difference yourself. The

Chapter 10 Is That All I Need to Know?

bottom line is that you must have flexibility in the knee to adjust to the situation, and going low on the board which slows you down can be useful to enhance your braking moves.

Why is this important in the turn?   The best explanation I have ever seen is in Chapter 37 of a book about skiing, *The Athletic Skier*, by Warren Witherell and David Evrard, published by The Athletic Skier Inc., Utah, 1993. Women don't need to have studied physics to understand centrifugal force because we all know that when the washing machine spins, the laundry flies away from the center outward to the sides of the tank. Think of the turn as the letter C and notice that there is an inside and outside area. At the top of the turn, gravity is pulling you down the hill, but centrifugal force compensates for this by pressuring you in the opposite uphill direction (just like the laundry). In the middle of the turn, you are in the fall line, with gravity causing you to pick up speed. At the end of the turn, you have gravity pulling you downhill and also centrifugal force as you are now on the outside of the C. The increased pressure of not one but two forces (gravity plus centrifugal) pulls you downward. That is why it is hard to control the board at the end of the turn, to slow down, and to tilt on edge. Instead, the board tends to *skid* leaving a banana peel track on the snow, rather than the sharp line we desire (as in a *carve*). Skidding diverts your forward motion by also going sideways. As such, it is an ineffective move.

Back to the subject of the knees. If one stands tall to start the turn there will be increased acceleration in a controlled body position. By lowering the body, bending the knees at the final part of the turn, one can counter the effect of gravity plus centrifugal force, thus reasserting control at this last phase. You won't have to apply the brakes by tilting the board so much on edge; it is simply done by bending the knees which lowers your body mass and slows you down. That is, until you rise up to initiate the next turn.

One other aspect of the bent knee story is that rather than thinking of the rising/sinking action in terms of unweighting, you should also be using your knees to retract the board. In other words, the knees become something like shocks on a car (or a mountain bike). Because trails are not usually totally smooth, stiff legged riders will be jolting their bodies each time they go over a rut, whereas those with flexible knees absorb these irregularities by drawing up the board. So, as they say, "Bend ze knees, pleeze."

Skidding Versus Carving

I took ski lessons for many years and always was admonished for "skidding" my turns. I dutifully apologized, although I never really had any idea what that meant nor how to correct it! That's the problem with technical vocabulary which snowsport pros tend to use and of which the public has no understanding. As explained above, there is a reason explained by physics which causes skidding, but perhaps it is simpler to explain the goal of the carve. Imagine a deeply carved letter C clearly delineated to show the path of your track in the snow through the turn. It's the difference between the skidded turn mark as if a spatula was used to spread icing on a cake compared to the sharp carved line of a knife (used to cut the cake slice). To accomplish this, the board must have been on a tilted edge all through, with a quick skip barely perceptible in the middle where you switched to the opposite edge. This is the goal. Think of one of those big city fire engines with a driver in front and another steering the back end; the board is your fire engine and it needs to be guided. In the midpoint of the turn you must steer the board by applying pressure to the tail end, forcing it to accept, on a tilt, the same line of travel as the front tilted edge has gone. Technically, this is described as employing torsional flex and thereby creating the carved turn. You need not know the vocabulary, but you should understand the objective. By cutting a clean line in the snow there is less drag on the board as it progresses forwards without simultaneously splaying out sideways as in the skid.   This is a more practical move than the skid which is awkward and simply is a sort of inefficient way to make a turn. You might not care whether you are losing speed, but skidded turns will absorb your energy, and they lack the grace of a smooth cutting slice through the snow surface. A perfect carve soon becomes every snowboarder's goal.

Bumps

This book is supposed to be a mere introduction to snowboarding, not a manual for advanced riders. However, once you are off the learning area, you will start to encounter bumped up snow surfaces. I once had an outraged student complain that the mountain should be ashamed of its grooming crew because the trail was not smooth. This was a person who had never before skied or snowboarded. He did not understand that bumps (moguls) are the result of skier/snowboarder turns where the snow gets pushed aside to the extent that it forms huge lumps which skiers have traditionally described in comparison to the size of Volkswagens.

There is a basic approach to riding bumps. First of all, you should have the proper attitude. If you look at the trail ahead as if you were in a pockmarked minefield and your life is in danger, you will not be very enthusiastic about your efforts to survive. Instead, tell yourself that the bumps are your friends. They are there to create a playground of fun. As to whether to go over or around, it sort of varies with the conditions (icy or soft snow, close together or far apart bumps, *etc.*). Ideally, as a beginner at this, you should approach the bump, ride up to its crest, do a pivot turn, then do a straight slide down the back. This is the simplest method of attack, but it will only work in the simplest least sophisticated of bumps. Once you have been able to cross the first bump, ride over the next few in an up and down traverse, and then try to change direction with another pivot turn. Usually, turning on about every three or four bumps is a good way to begin to learn mastery as it offers you time to reassert your balance and your brain. The key in attacking a bump field is to keep your weight forward. The instant that you tend to sit back, you will find yourself down and stuck cradled in the valley of the mogul. Watch for bumps to practice on during the early season so that by the time spring comes around and the snow is soft, you will have developed the skills to handle those heavily bumped up trails.

Riding Catwalks and the Flats

I have a cat who seldom ever loses his balance, even when racing across the slick surface of uncarpeted floors or on narrow ledges. He not only has four legs but also a tail which all contribute to his agility. We, on snowboards, simply have to do our best with what we have: sharp edges and quick reactions. Catwalks are trails which are too narrow to allow traverses or turns. They tend to be connecting paths joining the ski trails and therefore are usually well traveled. This means that they tend to be "skied off" in that the surface is slick from so much skier/snowboarder traffic.

On catwalks you won't always have room to do any turns, not only due to the narrowness of the trail but also because of the crowds of people. Therefore, the best thing is to travel on crossover trails with the 1-2-3 rhythm but always going back to the initial edge. You will be holding your tilted edge then changing to flat then reverting back to the same edge again. Be sure that you stay on the uphill or inside section of the ski trail, hugging the upper area rather than heading to the lower trail edge with the danger of going off the side into the woods!   Your only actual difficulty in these situations is the cramping of your muscles from holding onto one riding edge for so long a time. That is why you have to give your poor aching legs a break by momentarily allowing the board to go flat.

So many times we ride an entire trail only to have difficulty at the very end where the runoff is flat.   This is usually a situation where people simply underestimate the terrain challenge and tend to become distracted with the scene at the trail base. Here again is where the 1-2-3 rhythm is so essential in tilting the board by going from

1. first edge
2. to flat with no edging
3. to the opposite edge

but all done going straight ahead, not traversing.   Practice makes perfect.

Powder

You are in luck. The mountain has just received a gift from the heavens of over six inches of fresh powder. Western

Snowboarding for Women

skiers have powder days all the time; Eastern skiers treasure the occasions. For first lesson snowboarders, powder conditions are truly a blessing mostly because they can't really do anything wrong. No matter how a person leans, the snow gently supports the board. That's why we instructors call it "ego snow." These are perfect conditions for learning: not too fast a surface and all movements are cushioned with errors forgiven. The only problem is going to be tomorrow when the groomers have packed down the snow. Then it will make a difference which edge of the board is tilted, and speed must be controlled. Second day snowboarders are always puzzled by their tremendous degree of success in the freshies just twenty-four hours ago, and now everything they do seems to be the wrong move. That was because the powder made all corrections for them; today the rider must do so.

For Eastern riders, powder often causes a perceptual problem. We are so used to a hard pack surface that the vision of soft clumped snow causes our brains to react with warning. We simply are not accustomed to heaps of undulating surface which we can go straight through. The strategy I apply in these situations is to keep repeating to myself the words "whipped cream" to remind me that this is light and fluffy, and I can go into it without restraint.

The other way people have problems is because with a big dump of snow, one has to allow the board to float. Your bindings may disappear from sight, and the board will sink deep into the snow which tends to make some people react with anxiety. What you must do is allow the board to float through the powder with your upper body rising and sinking, causing weighting and unweighting. It is imperative to keep the nose (front end) of the board pointing upward, rather than

140

allowing it to sink. To enhance this, some riders like to move their binding positions back slightly or even keep on hand another snowboard which is longer in length, specifically for use after a big dump. Turns must be very round, never sharp, and knees must do the work Your mental image should be to go light as a bunny as you actually bounce your way down the trail. It's a heady feeling that's just wonderful!

A word of caution: do not get carried away by the excitement of all that powder and venture off the marked trail in violation of ski resort regulations and the Responsibility Code (Chapter 7). Every season snowboarders drown in tree wells. Do not become one of those statistics.

Ice

Eastern riders all wish for powder days but we must learn to live with ice. Ice comes in different variations: blue ice, bullet proof ice, or those large frozen chunks called"death cookies." It's a fact of life that, even with the best grooming machines which crunch up the frozen surface into frozen granular, you will still risk encounters with ice. First of all, don't panic. Simply focus your eyes on the nearest place where there is snow cover and head for it. If you were driving your car and suddenly saw ice ahead, what would you do? Would you jam on the brakes? Certainly not! The same concept applies to snowboarding. Heavy edging will cause serious skidding and an out of control situation. Instead, gain confidence in that your snowboard has sharp edges (a good thing to have checked out at a tuning shop before setting out onto icy conditions), and allow that knife sharp edge to do its job. Think of the car braking image; cars steer into the path of a skid. Snowboarders should steer the tail edge of their board in the same path that the front edge has traveled. Recognize that move? You should be doing a carve.

Another reminder of how we cope with ice in everyday life is to think about how women get out of a car when in an icy parking lot, particularly when wearing high heeled shoes. True, we tend to walk gingerly, but decisively. We are light on our feet, almost tiptoeing, and we look ahead to where it is safe to proceed. There is never a hard pushing on the heel or jamming down of the foot. Think of your board and its edges as a sharp knife slicing vertically downward rather than pushing horizontally across a surface. Follow these logical steps in terms of avoiding the horizontal skid by applying the cutting edge via the carve and moving decisively but cautiously to safety. With an understanding of these moves, you should not ever allow yourself to be intimidated by the conditions. In fact, when you hear the loud scream of your board cutting into the icy surface it should actually give you a sense of empowerment.

Poor Visibility

You've purchased your lift ticket, you are ready to ride, but you can't see the mountain! This is really a personal call, but I suggest going into the lodge and making new friends. It is hard enough to find your way on a ski mountain without being blindfolded by fog. Even those who are familiar with the ski area will attest to the fact that fog is disorienting. You really can't tell uphill from downhill, and sound is so distorted that you don't know how close you are to other people on the trail.

Heavy snow is also similar to fog in that you will find yourself proceeding in a blind situation. Experienced skiers

Chapter 10 Is That All I Need to Know?

and boarders know that sticking close to the edge of the trail along the tree line offers definition, but obviously, this also offers high risk of error and a danger of going off the trail into those trees!   Conditions can vary within the ski resort itself. For example, at my home mountain of Killington we have six interconnected mountains. At any time one of them (usually Bear Mountain) may be in full sunshine while another (Killington Peak) is totally obscured due to the weather conditions. Check trail maps and ask for guidance at the ski school or resort concierge desk. Just keep in mind my personal motto: If you can't see it, don't ski it.

11
You're Committed

By now we should have reached your goal. The purpose was to get you to venture forth into the world of snowsports and to offer yourself the experience of snowboarding. It wasn't easy, but you have passed the trials of initiation. You love to snowboard, and this is in spite of the fact that you probably still don't like the cold weather, don't do well with heights, and don't like to go too fast. None of that matters anymore. You have learned how to dress, you are brave about the chair lifts, and you have mastered control of your board.

An unexpected bonus is to have known the serenity of the mountain landscape hushed with snow and experienced the beauty of nature first hand along with a newfound respect for the mountain environment and understanding of winter's challenges. You are out there having loads of fun with your friends plus meeting new people.   In essence, becoming a snowboarder has opened up a new world for you in which you will be checking weather forecasts, clipping out articles on ski/snowboard resorts, watching for airline discounts, and spending your summer months waiting for winter.

Purchasing Your Own Equipment

At this stage, it would be advisable to go back and re-

read Chapter 5 which deals with hard equipment before getting involved in the more complex discussion which follows here. We look for certain elements when renting, but making a purchase certainly requires deeper analysis. In fact, if you are afraid that your patience will be exhausted with the variety of choices to be herein presented in equipment selection, be patient.

Did you ever read Herman Melville's *Moby Dick?* Aside from the plot of a megalomaniac sea captain in pursuit of the white whale called Moby Dick, there is one chapter devoted to whale classification, another on parts of the whale, then discussion of whales as they appear in art, another section on habits of whales, a discourse on whiteness itself...you get the general idea. Obviously, this book is not attempting to emulate a literary classic, yet Melville's book sets an example of explicitness in the understanding of a subject. I repeat; be patient in your reading of this chapter. Do not skip it. You will benefit from the advantage of knowing your extensive range of options before you are in the distracting environment of a retail snowboard shop.

Boots

By now you should be really committed to the sport of snowboarding. In fact, I'm rather surprised that it took so long (many of my clinic guests purchase their own equipment after the very first day of lessons). The initial item for you to consider buying would be boots. You can read all the advertisements, notice the brands which other snowboarders are wearing, and ask the salespeople at snowboard shops, but the bottom line is that the boot simply has to be the right fitting boot for <u>you</u>. Name brands are recommended based on their reputations, and a good snowboard shop will guide you to the best purchase in terms of warmth and dryness. Remember that the money saved on a "special" will be of little comfort when you are out there with cold feet from damp boots or feel the chaffing effect of a poor fit.

What is a good fit? You should be trying on boots with the specific socks which you will be wearing when snowboarding. If not, you would be wise to purchase snowboarding socks now before proceeding further. Buy several pairs because you will need them to wear with the boots on trips lasting more than one day. In case you were planning to do nightly handwash, don't count on it because they never dry in time. As stated in Chapter 5 regarding general equipment issues, the boot should be snug and comfortable. Your heel should be firmly in place without gross slippage upwards. Walk around the store (hopefully you will have allowed quite a bit of time for this shopping project), leaning forward and backward, from toe to heel, then try rolling your toes from big toe to little toe. If the boot is truly comfortable then you will be assured of having proper blood circulation, and your feet will be warm.

Most snowboard boot companies now have lines designed specifically for women. Aside from being appealing in terms of looks, these boots tend to be better fitting than the unisex models. Women often have narrow heels which leads to rubbing in the ankle area when the heel tends to lift out of place. Some of us have feet which turn inward (pronation), others turn outward, arch heights vary, *etc.* We are all different, and these differences can be crucial in selecting the proper fitting boot.

I recently purchased a boot which was a comfortable

fit, but turned out not to be warm enough (remember in my introduction: I am always colder than most people). My local Killington resource was at Peak Performance, a ski shop, where board certified pedorthist David Strousse offered me a creative solution. He switched the liner (the removable part of the boot separate from the outer shell) of my snowboard boot and substituted it with a super warm liner from a ski boot. The result is my own unique hybrid of a ski boot liner matched with the step-in snowboard boot necessary for coordination with my binding system. It works.

A good boot fitter can do a lot. There are heel or ankle lifts and padding of all sorts. As stated in my own case, liners can be adjusted or even exchanged, and pressure spots can be eliminated. That, in itself, is the most important reason to shop where skilled boot fitters are on the job. It's like selecting a good medical specialist. Choose a person who does his specialty exclusively, not someone with a general practice

The best boot fitters are found at the most popular ski areas where they therefore have the most exposure to fitting problems or are located at a quality (usually large city) ski shop. Look for the America's Best Bootfitters emblem on display, or go to their Web site at www.bootfitters.com for a listing of the shops which employ certified boot fitters. Another source of recommendation is the ski school. Ask your instructor for a recommendation. Chip Dwyer from Northern Ski Works regularly gives talks on boot fitting to our Women's Turn group, a special program at Killington for women skiers and snowboarders. Also, as in my personal experience, do not limit yourself to only patronizing snowboard shops. Experienced ski shop bootfitters have been around for a very long time, and boots are boots, no matter how they function.

Chapter 11 You're Committed

A really good thing to have are custom footbeds, even if you do not have glaring boot fit problems. The footbed assures proper alignment which will create better balance when out on the hill. These are not the expensive medical orthotics you might have in mind. They are custom molded innersoles and are not overly costly or particularly complicated to have made. Ski/snowboard shops have special equipment which creates the footbed when you stand on a machine upon special innersoles. These become shaped in response to heat application. It doesn't take long to create the impression, and once you have them made, they will last through the lifetimes of several pairs of boots.

Remember that, as the saying goes, your ride depends on "where the tire hits the road." Your boot fit is crucial to proper snowboard movement and balance because the boot provides the first link between the body movement of your foot by way of the binding to the board itself. The best on snow performance is predicated upon response from your feet, so skillful riding really starts back in the sales section of the snowboard shop when you select your boots.

For those who like to check these things out via the Internet, Jeannie Thoren is a competitive skier who has developed a footbed product designed specifically for women. "The weak link in a woman's skiing is usually her equipment," reads the opening statement posted on the Web at www.jeanniethoren.com. She has designed a performance insole which has a built-in heel lift. Although her product was engineered for women who ski, the snowboarding woman has the same boot fit adjustment problem. This product might be the answer for you. You can also contact Jeannie at jeanthoren@aol.com.

Now that you are purchasing boots, it is a good idea to buy some sort of a boot dryer. There was mention in Chapter 5 of the fact that feet perspire, and the insides of your boots will be quite damp by the end of the day. Unless you take serious measures to remedy the wet boot situation, you will be a very unhappy person tomorrow morning if you must start the day with cold damp boots. There are numerous boot dryer products on the market, and your best place to seek them out is at a ski area where you can shop around. For a number of years I have been using a system made by Evaporator which blows cool air. It has a total of four outlets with varied size nozzles to dry either two sets of boots or one set of boots and a pair of gloves. The unit even comes in a miniature hatbox style case which is perfect for travel. Another less expensive system I have found handy is Happy Feet, a set of rods which conduct heat. Minimal in design, they do the job. Using a hair dryer is always available as a last resort, but purchasing a boot dryer is certainly the wiser way to go.

Board

Selecting a snowboard can definitely be a mystifying proposition. There are so many companies who make snowboards, and many among these models are designed specifically for women. The best way to start is with a product catalog. If you have looked at the sales rack of a snowboard shop or studied any company brochure, you will be aware that there are many choices offered in snowboard design, and this does not refer merely to the graphics. Dependent upon the rider's ability skills, they range from entry level (beginner) boards to those for advanced or expert riders. Handling and performance are influenced by internal composition, *flex* (how easily the board bends or twists), board shape, and basic construction.

You can eliminate certain boards simply by using the criteria of how experienced you are and what type of riding you choose to do: whether you want to race, do freestyle in the half pipe and tricks in a snowboard park, or prefer what is called all mountain riding. If you are going to concentrate on racing, then you will want to focus on selections among racing boards with a hard boot and clamp binding set up. All mountain riding, versus freestyle, offers a wide range of selection as many boards are suitable for crossover activity, and here you will also have to make a binding (and boot) decision between step-in or buckle.

Once you have determined which to eliminate based on the category of riding ability, the first thing to consider is length. Boards are measured in centimeters which is hard for Americans who have never succumbed to mastering the metric system. Therefore, the seemingly slight variation of the board measurements tend not to have a lot of meaning for us. In general, when set up standing in front of you, the board should come somewhere in the area zone between your shoulder and your nose. Not too scientific. Fortunately there are charts (usually on a sticker attached to the board base) specifying weight range for the varied size boards.

Desirable length varies in terms of where you plan to ride. For example, if you are headed for the park, your freestyle board should be near shoulder height because shorter boards are quicker to turn. On the other hand, if you are going free riding (general all mountain riding), you will want something a bit longer, closer to or above your chin when the board is standing on its tail. An additional factor to consider in selecting length is whether you will be doing a lot of powder riding which does well with a longer board.

The real problem with choosing is because the various boards are actually quite different. Since they do not have the same internal construction, they will ride quite differently, even if they are of equal length. Some boards are designed to ride forward only, whereas others go easily in both directions, forward and back. This is referred to as *directionality*. The all mountain or free riding boards can work well doing park and pipe, but usually spend most of their riding time down mountain trails. They are engineered to go smoothly in one direction but can offer the versatility of still being able to ride switch. For the freestyler, in terms of board orientation, there is no difference which direction you are headed. Frontwards is also backwards. That is why the twin tip boards were developed.

Board shape is a concern. It's easy to understand the value of those twin tip boards if you are doing spins and tricks or hanging out in the halfpipe. They offer the ability to ride the same in either direction and have duplicate head /tail shaping. The *nose* (front) is the same shape as the *tail* (back). In such a situation you would then also want a board with snap so that you can pop off the tail doing ollies. You will certainly want a quick responding board for sudden moves and a solid platform for landings after jumps, if all that is in your plans for the future.

The very best way to make a judgement is to "demo" a board. These are the sample boards available for demonstration (rental cost is usually applied to purchase price). The problem will be that of available inventory in finding one of the correct length for your body weight and riding ability. In any event, one can still get an idea of how the board reacts, even if it is not a perfect fit. Snowboard shop salespeople use language you won't really understand, for example, the meaning of what is a stiff board or a "noodle," and how some boards are "more forgiving." An understanding of the elements of a snowboard will help. Otherwise, these are just words without meaning for you. Hang in there, because here comes some more technical stuff to better prepare you!

Length has been mentioned, but there are other measurements. The waist width (size at the narrowest part where bindings are placed) is always given. This is crucial for people with larger boot sizes as a narrow waist will result in toe or heel drag. A board with a narrow waist will require the extreme angles of a very aggressive stance for the binding, as seen in racing boards (which are used with hard boot setup). The wider waist board lacks the quickness of turning power but in compensation will have additional stability and give an easier ride.

Then, there are the elements of *sidecut* and also *effective edge.* Think of turn shape on the snow as an outline from the edge of a circle. The sidecut radius is in direct proportion to the radius of that circle. Another way to explain it is that the silhouetted shape of the board, the effective edge, is the edge area that actually touches the snow. That is what influences the actual shape of your turns as a result of its sidecut. If you make short radius turns (advanced riders), you want a board with smaller sidecut radius resulting in a decreased sidecut which enacts a sharper turn. This may not be so noticeable to your untutored eye, but the sidecut is dramatically illustrated when looking at the extremely pronounced shape of the racing board, enabling it to fly past the gates with sharp turns. Those who prefer larger longer turns will go for the increased sidecut . In essence, the larger the radius, the larger the circle, and the more mellow the turns.

Effective edge is really the more realistic measure of board length as it refers to how much of the metal edge of the board actually comes in contact with the snow. You can feel the difference when riding boards of different effective edge as the more edge touching snow, the more controlled ride you will have. Of course, you don't really use all of that edge from nose to tail anyway. When making the turn, the very front tip area of the board will not come into play, but the concave arc of the side is what contacts the snow surface when pressure is applied to the board. In fact, when purchasing your board, be sure to have the shop "detune" the nose of the board some five to six inches down on each side so that it will not grab as you initiate a turn.

The shop salesperson may lean the board against a wall and push against it to show the bendability. We call this *flex*. Boards must have enough flex to bend while you ride them without breaking, sort of like a shock absorber. A beginning snowboarder will find it difficult to make turns on a stiff board. Keep in mind your body weight as a factor, and that softer boards are more forgiving for less experienced and lighter weight riders. Softer flex allows those nice C shaped turns for general all mountain riding. Stiff boards may be great in the bumps or doing jumps, but will you be going there? Flex is enacted both from nose to tail of the board along its length, and also one speaks of torsional flex which is twisting, so crucial in making carved turns.

Unless having the experience of doing a demo, you will have to rely upon the snowboard company's written materials and the salesperson to judge the importance of these elements in your situation, all in conjunction with your riding ability. Usually, the more advanced the rider, the more she wants the board to do, hence the requirement for a stiffer board. Again, ability level, terrain selection, and weight are key factors.

All people ride differently, and the perfect board for your friend will not necessarily suit you. I once purchased a board which came very highly recommended not only in trade magazines but also from another instructor. Unfortunately, as is commonly the case, the demo available was not the length I needed (too long) so I had attributed my less than perfect ride to the need for a different size. I bought the board anyway, convinced by so many endorsements, just ordering it in a shorter length. My mistake was that the company's product guide range of weight was rather broad, and my 105 pounds was really a bit too light to sufficiently handle the stiff construction. I eventually adjusted, but it certainly took a conscious effort. Since then I have found the board which works the best for me and each season order the latest model. Brand loyalty.

Camber is a word you may hear which is the term used to describe the stored energy latent in a board. You may notice that when placed flat on the floor, the center section has a slight rise. Sometimes this is more easily visible with skis. When a ski or snowboard turns, it goes into reverse camber, and the rise becomes akin to a pivot point pressuring downward. In essence, the more camber, the more lively is the board and the quicker responding. Too much camber can be hard to handle; slightly less camber can provide a more leisurely ride. After extensive usage, advanced age, or poor care, the camber will disappear, and a snowboard will lose its liveliness. A dead response to your riding movements will send you the message that it is now time to shop for a replacement. Snowboard catalogs will give you a full explanation of the uniqueness of their product's board construction. Think of the board as a series of layers with filler between the base and top sheet. I know that it is hard to commit to purchasing a board with an unappealing top or bottom graphic, but you really must consider the importance of that which cannot be seen. The inner construction is what creates the snap and power of a board and allows it to give a signature ride. The choice of *sandwich* versus *cap* design refers to the sealing in of the material between the outermost layers. Cap construction wraps the entire package in fiberglass up to the metal edges, whereas sandwich stacks the interior layers and then covers the edges with a sidewall. What goes inside? Usually different types of fiberglass ,wood, resin or types of foam. They all make a substantial difference which is why there are so many snowboard brand choices.

Notice that I have <u>not</u> specifically mentioned a single snowboard manufacturer or given any Web sites. That is primarily because there so very many companies who are making so many styles of boards for so many different types of terrain with the additional variant of suitability for different conditions (*ie.* powder vs. hardpack). Then, within those categories are the board companies which have special lines just for women, and some even offer a variety therein. The other problem is that the board your friend loves to ride is not necessarily the board you will enjoy. The board I like may be one you would hate!

The very best way to narrow your selection is to rely upon the experts. Usually in the month of October, snowboarding magazines such as *Snowboard Life, Snowboarder Magazine,* or *Transworld Snowboarding* have an issue rating their choice of the top snowboards for the upcoming season. It's the business of professionals to know what is really good. Take their advice as opposed to that of a shop eager to unload its inventory. Then study the company catalogs, be honest in your self evaluation of riding ability, try to arrange a demo, and make your best judgement call. Good luck.

Bindings

This is just a reminder that your bindings will be determined first of all by whether you are going the hard boot or soft boot route. Then, if a soft boot, it really becomes a matter of step-in versus buckle. Refer back to the discussion of this issue in Chapter 5, and remember that the most important factor is boot fit. You may want to have a certain step-in, but the boot must be compatible with the binding, and if the boot is not comfortable, then you really cannot consider that binding. That is the twinning problem of step-ins in that each binding system works only with the company's matched boot.

Buckle bindings offer more flexibility in that you select your boot based on comfort and fit and then decide, mostly based on your bank account balance, which manufacturer's binding to purchase. Some snowboarding companies now offer binding systems that are specifically designed for women. Bindings are really important as they form the reaction link from your boot-enclosed foot to the board. For this reason I tend to advise going for the best that you can afford. Price can be a way to help determine quality. Consider what you expect from the binding in relation to what type of snowboarding you plan on doing (*ie*. halfpipe, freestyle, *etc*.). Before sealing the deal, be absolutely sure that your boot fits easily in and out of the binding plate and also that you understand completely the mechanisms involved.

Highbacks Versus Lowbacks

When making a heelside turn, as you now know, you must go forward pressuring with the ankle. This move requires some sort of a support: hence, the piece which rises vertically from the back at the heel end of the binding. Initially, these *highback* supports were designed about 8 inches high. Then came the impact of skateboarders upon snowboard engineering and the result was a *lowback*, only half the size, which was more stylish looking and particularly popular with young freestyle riders.   Highback vs. lowback became something of a hot issue with some preferring the less obtrusive device whereas others differed in opinion, even among freestylers, some of whom argued that the highback assists in getting air because it offers necessary support to the calf of the leg when one goes up the wall of the halfpipe. That may not be far up there on your list of requirements, but the advantage of a highback, along with offering support on the heelside turn, is the forward lean   adjustment.   If you play around with different positions you will become aware of its role in guiding you on those heelside turns. Low backs seem to be out of style by now anyway.

The highbacks of step-in bindings can be exposed (external) or they are incorporated into the boot which is required to match the set up. When trying on boots with internal highbacks, ask the sales person about the forward lean adjustments. As stated above and earlier in Chapter 5, there are two advantages of an external highback. One is that of ease in forward lean adjustment and the second, perhaps more important element, is that of having the stiff highback on the board rather than inside the boot which certainly makes for a great deal more comfort when walking in your snowboard boots. Leave that stiff backing on the board itself rather than rising up from the heel area inside your boot.

Care of Your New Purchases

Ski areas offer season tunes or you can pay as you go, but for most people it is helpful (and financially prudent) to know something of caring for the equipment yourself. There are two areas of maintenance in regard to the snowboard: the edges and the base.

Edges should be sharp, especially as you want them to hold you on icy surfaces. The problem with doing the edges yourself is that, unless you really know what you are doing, you can destroy the bevel. It's not like trimming your bangs because you hadn't time to go to the beauty parlor. Hair grows back, but snowboard edges that are filed off will have that metal gone forever. It is not difficult to learn how to deburr those rough snags on the edges. It is advisable to have an experienced friend or shop tuner demonstrate for you the use of a stone to deburr, but leave it in the shop to have edges done when they are in need of sharpening.

Taking care of the base is another story. First of all, it helps to understand the role of wax. Movement of a board over the snow surface creates friction which results in heat, causing snow particles to melt into droplets of water upon the board base. Bad enough that the wetness slows you down, but then these drops refreeze and clump up during the time that

Snowboarding for Women

they move along towards the tail of the board. Wax is what allows you to slide since it reduces the friction and prevents water adhesion to the snowboard base.

Ski and snowboard racers are the gurus of waxing. Their success depends not only upon their skill in riding a course but also in selecting the wax which will help them go the fastest. For the rest of us, knowledge of the basic categories will suffice. You should have wax sticks of the basic color trio: yellow for warmest temperatures ($32°$), red for warm ($27°$), and green for cold ($16°-0°$).

Gather up the following items necessary to do a tuning:

1. an old sheet or tablecloth to use as a dropcloth because wax shavings will fall to the floor
2. the least expensive most basic iron you can find
3. a triangle shaped scraper and citrus cleaner, purchased at a ski/snowboard shop
4. some clean rags for use with the citrus cleaner
5. Scotch-Brite pads (buy at a supermarket)

Spread the dropcloth on the floor and get set to become a tuning-tech.

Step #1: Lay the board flat either on the floor or propped up between two chairs, and clean the base. Using a triangle shaped scraper you will be able to pull off some of the old wax, going from tip to tail. Then use the citrus cleaner which will remove the remaining old wax and any dirt.

Step #2: Heat your iron at most on medium setting, and, holding the wax stick perpendicular to it, allow dribbles of wax to drop down onto the board. Generously create a modern art style abstract pattern of wax polka dots over the entire base surface. Think Jackson Pollock.

Step #3: This is the easy part for most women. With a low to medium setting (you don't want to scorch the surface), lightly iron the board. <u>You must keep the iron moving</u> as you gloss over those drops of wax, spreading them onto a smooth surface across the base (trying not to coat the metal edges).

Step #4: Allow the wax to cool and harden. This will take at least 20-30 minutes, or preferably, let it sit overnight.

Step #5: You did such a nice job ironing on all that wax. Now it is necessary to scrape it off. Using that triangle shaped scraper, pull towards you, working vertically from tip to the tail area.

Step #6: Using either a Scotch-Brite pad (those large green squares) or even a scouring sponge (no soap), polish the base. Again, movement should not be circular but vertical, from tip to tail.

It's a good idea to gather together these tuning items and assemble a little kit similar to your personal travel cosmetics bag. You will appreciate its existence if you happen to go on vacation and experience sudden extreme temperature changes. A board with the wrong wax will not glide. It barely moves at all. Another option is to pack a tin of snowboard wax along with an application sponge and wiping cloth. That will give you a quick fix without getting involved in a waxing project. Either way, check out the necessary materials needed for waxing before the crisis situation arises. On the other hand, even if you are really good at doing the wax routine, you should occasionally take the board to a shop for a professionally done job. Gouges and deep scrapes from rocky or debris ridden trails require sophisticated treatment and know-how for proper repair. You will learn to appreciate the importance of a good waxing to insure a smooth ride along with the tuned board's sharpened edges for firm holding on icy slopes.

Off Season Storage

Heat rises. Therefore an attic is the warmest part of a house and not a happy place for winter sport equipment. Instead, select a cool dry area for off season storage. Clean your boots, dry them inside and out, stuff with paper towel (this keeps out spiders), lace, and buckle them up. If you are really a neatie, you may want to store your boots in a container to keep them free of what will be a six month layer of surface dust.

The board requires a bit more effort. Remember the wax instructions? Follow steps 1-4. What you want now is an extra heavy coat of protective wax which will sit on the board until you scrape it off a half year later. If you haven't mastered the ironing technique or haven't had the board tuned during the season, this would be a good time to drop it off at a shop, have the edges done, the base checked out, and let them give it that heavy wax coating. Either way, with this minimal end of season care, you will be ready to go come the earliest flurries of next winter.

Wash your outerwear jacket and snowboard pants, remembering that even though powder leaves a residue, it is preferable over liquid soap which takes away water repellence. Just for good measure, be sure to spray with Scotch-Guard. An excellent product I have used is Red Wash. To quote the bottle, "No, dummy, it doesn't turn your clothes red. " By its attitude, one tends to assume it is a snowboard product. Distribution may be local only, as the label states manufacture in Burlington, VT. At any rate, it is effective for cleaning down filled and synthetic insulated garments. Another product you can look for is Revivex, developed by the makers of Gore-tex fabric. "Specifically engineered for Gore-tex, Activent, and Dryloft products," this spray will restore water repellent finishes. Go to them on the Web at www.gorefabrics.com for dealer listings in your region.

That's it! You have learned about snowboarding from start to finish, from first purchases to final details. Now that the season is over, be sure that you use the time off constructively. Let's be honest with ourselves, and instead of just focusing on what a great time you had snowboarding, remember how stiff you were after the first day out on the hill. The calves of your legs ached, and your arms were weary from lugging around the board. You had muscle pain from muscles you didn't know existed! Here is your chance. Use the off season months to really get into shape. Join a health club, have a regimen of walking, go to group aerobics, start running, try biking, do rock climbing, try wind surfing. Read about the benefits for women of all ages to do weights, and buy yourself a set of dumbbells. What is really being implied here is that because of your snowboarding, you have initiated a different lifestyle. You may never have thought of yourself as athletic or an outdoors person, certainly never someone who loved winter weather. Unexpectedly, you now have a use for the warmer months as a period of readiness for what has now become your focus season. You should be motivated to indulge yourself in a newly revised self image, all because you have attained your goal of learning to snowboard.

Congratulations, Betty Shred!

Just who are those Betty Shreds, anyway?

12
Who Snowboards?

As you must have realized by now, one need not want to be an Olympic hopeful to decide to snowboard. Nor do you have to envision yourself flying up the sides of a halfpipe or riding staircase railings. You certainly don't have to be a teenager. In fact, *The New York Times* has referred to the sport's age shift to mature riders as "the greying of snowboarding." And "greys on trays" is the teenagers' lament for a sport which no longer draws exclusively from their group.

Asking women who ride about what enticed them to become involved provides varied and interesting answers. One woman acquaintance said that her family had a country house in Vermont so she had skied, that is, until injuring her knee. Taking time out caring for her young children and strengthening her knee, she then decided that taking the family skiing involved too much equipment and had chosen snowboarding simply because there would be less to carry. It sounded like a funny reason, but when you think about it, skiers must juggle four times the equipment compared to that of a boarder. They have two skis and a set of poles, none of which are easy to carry especially when attempting to walk in those stiff ungainly ski boots. Fashion also played a major role for this person as she made an additional comment that she really loved the style of snowboard clothing. Those may not be the elements which the snowboard industry would like to publicize as the draw for the sport, but it reflects an honest dose of reality as to what this one woman found attractive about snowboarding. She is not a single voice in that respect.

I recently coached an introductory lesson which was shared between a husband and wife. Nancy later told me that she had invited Bob along because she "didn't want to do it alone," but she was the person who was motivated to snowboard due to a desire to learn this new snowsport. Having skied since early childhood, it simply had lost its allure for her: "When you've done something regularly even at different mountains for over forty years, it gets boring." She had tried telemark skiing but found it too difficult, too much work, and rough on the knees. Her attraction to snowboarding? "Snowboarding looks very graceful, flowing, and has a sense of freedom to it." Other motivating factors for her were those soft boots and the ease of less equipment to carry around. Sounds like familiar reasons to sign up.

One nice thing about being an instructor is that you teach people who then become your friends. In fact, I am encouraging Sasha to take the instructor's course and join me on staff, yet she too, as I did, had a seemingly unpromising time entering into snowboarding. "It was brutal...I persevered though, and am happy with my progress. I didn't get it after one, two, or three days, but all the talk about the learning curve is true. I remember always thinking skiing was work with moments of 'W*hee*, this is fun!' few and far between. In contrast, snowboarding is one long constant *wheeee* all the way down the mountain! Snowboarding is thrilling, challenging, and can be a meditative experience too. Snowboarding has made me love the winter. I can't wait for the instructor's

Chapter 12 Who Snowboards?

course."

When I attended the adult session of High Cascade Snowboard Camp at Mt. Bachelor, Oregon, I became friends with Polly. She is an instructor from a ski area in the state of Washington and had signed up for the camp, as I did, to improve riding and half pipe skills. She too had once been a skier until she had an introductory snowboarding lesson from (in her words) "one of my heroes, Scott Erickson, former National Demo Team member, also one of the planet's best snowboarders." She "was hooked because of the ability to express myself, my freedom to be who I really am on the snow, the absolute fun of it all." Polly and I both did the same exact thing; we stopped skiing and never looked back.

Polly teaches snowboarding as training director for Ski Masters and states that she is "stoked on teaching other people how to ride...women, especially-- setting them free, watching them gain courage, skill, freedom, being stoked also, letting them know that they can do this too, not just 'the guys', and giving them the chance to feel the grace and beauty of snowboarding." Although we live on opposite coasts of the United States, the two of us both certainly speak the same exact language (including the snowboard vernacular of "stoked") in describing what is so special about snowboarding and why we really care about introducing women to our sport.

My friend Indira works for NGO Working Group on Women, Peace and Security which, when she is not snowboarding, takes her all over the world attending conferences on women's issues. She pointed out to me as an appealing aspect of being a snowboarder is the knowledge that the industry's biggest women stars are involved in the annual fund-raising Snowboarding for Breast Cancer at Squaw Valley

Snowboarding for Women

Resort. I am well aware of this because the snowboard I ride is the Feelgood designed by Shannon Dunn for Burton Snowboards whose catalog states that "Shannon donates a portion of her Feelgood royalties to the Boarding for Breast Cancer Foundation.

Indira sees the rising number of women who snowboard as an aspect of what she perceives to be "gender equality...women who learn how to ride tend to like to be as good as their partners. Look around and you will see that the snowboard Betties take charge of their own image as opposed to the ski bunnies. For example, look at the snowboard catalogs. The clothing for women is made by women who ride." An interesting aspect of her commentary was the fact that, having come to the United States from the recent Yugoslavia, she enjoyed learning snowboarding not only because of seeking a kid's idea of fun at the age of twenty-nine but also as a "sense of belonging to [this, her] newly acquired culture in the United States."

Tabitha instructs with me at Killington, and she commented that she started to snowboard when she was only eleven years old, attracted by doing something different. That's the counter culture appeal of snowboarding which is very quickly disappearing as the sport has become so mainstream. Although, noting her goggles with spikes protruding, one is reminded that, no matter how the numbers of riders increase, this is still a group which allows lots of personal space for individualism in attitude, clothing, and general demeanor.

Pansy is one of my most enthusiastic snowboarding friends. When I asked her why she took up snowboarding, she reminded me that, as a skier with a history of five knee surgeries, the doctor said, "No more skiing!" What is snowboarding's lure for her? "I love a good challenge and to me that is what snowboarding is all about. It's never the same ride twice! There is something to do different every run down, be it working on a skill, hitting a jump, or just relaxing and enjoying the feel of the board beneath you. It's a sport that lets you be yourself on the slope, not to mention that you wear clothing that is hip, your board has cool designs [her board actually has a small bouquet of pansies on it], and everything about you on the slope is a reflection of the *real you.*" I told you that she was very enthusiastic. See what I mean?

I like to work with Betsy who is another instructor in our snowboard department at Killington (rather appropriately named The Perfect Turn Department). She is not only a good friend but also was the inspiration for my pigtailed Betty Shred drawings. Betsy apologizes for sounding dramatic, but has described her feelings snowboarding as akin to a Zen experience: "I snowboard because I love the feeling of freedom and wellbeing that it gives me. Finessing my way down a beautiful snowy trail on a crisp winter day accompanied by the sound of wind in the trees gives me a sense of peace that can only be found on the board." As to coaching women, she comments that "there are still relatively so few women in the sport which makes it our duty, as female instructors, to bring more women in and show them what a great opportunity it is for all of us. Furthermore, snowboarding is the perfect sport for women because there are no dividing lines between the sexes. Everyone on the board is of equal status. In fact, it is also empowering for women to be on a level playing field in one of the sports where we can easily dominate." Betsy obviously must have agreed with my last "answer" for the shirt described in Chapter 1!

Snowboarding for Women

Over the years I have taught more people to snowboard who then came on staff than any of our other snowboard coaches at Killington. Michelle is the latest to join my list. I had coached her in our Woman's Turn program and then with private lessons, convincing her to come instruct at Killington where she worked last season in our kids' department. She enjoys teaching children, particularly little girls, because "I am a role model for them. Snowboarding is such a male dominated sport that I think it is important for women to get out there and ride and teach, showing girls that snowboarding is for them, not just for their brothers." She goes on to add that she sees herself as "a positive person in a young girl's life, encouraging them to succeed, a motivating factor which they will carry with them into future endeavors." For Michelle, as others, snowboarding is about more than merely taking part in a seasonal sport.

It becomes clear that snowboarding is a sport particularly appealing to women in terms of its grace, balance, fluidity, and, yes, it has a calm serenity of motion (once you are past the learning stage, that is). The fact that the clothing is attractive and the equipment user friendly sort of completes an already very positive picture. Snowboarding allows the rider to seek her own style with a sense of independence and individuality.

On the other hand, just how inclusive is the open invitation to learn to snowboard? My friend Lisa is a good example of a person with a physical disability who has embraced the sport of snowboarding. As a deaf person, she tends to have a major advantage over most with her disability in that she lip reads well. She had been a skier active in the U.S. Deaf Ski and Snowboard Association (USDSSA) when she met some snowboarders who invited her to join them in Vermont and learn to snowboard. Unfortunately, their only instruction was "just balance yourself." It resulted in the fact that she was "pretty much by myself all day, falling mostly!" But she persevered and three years later, as a member of the United States Olympic Deaf Snowboard Team, Lisa placed first in all of the qualifying events (the Slalom, GS, and halfpipe). From that dubious experience teaching herself to snowboard, she went on in 1999 to represent the United States in competition at the 14th World Winter Games for the Deaf held in Davos, Switzerland. Twenty-three nations competed, and Lisa returned home with a silver medal in the GS and a bronze in the Dual Slalom. Pretty impressive.

Lisa points out the frustrating situation of communication for most deaf people who need to receive instruction by way of sign language. She says that "at the Deaf Ski Conventions, there are deaf skiers and snowboarders who volunteer their time to provide instruction which is fee based and the money then donated to the Deaf Ski Organization. While this is a generous service, the problem is that these instructors are not professionally qualified." On the other hand, she adds that "many ski resorts have programs for people with disabilities and ski/snowboard instructors who will volunteer their time to teach, but unfortunately those organizations lack people with sign language skills."

Lisa had commented that "many people with disabilities feel out of place when trying to take on something new, so having others that are the same around you rebuilds confidence in learning a new sport." For this reason, she suggested seeking out programs for the disabled which provide instructions and social opportunities in snowboarding. The best resource for

Snowboarding for Women

listings of resort instruction for the disabled is to go to the Web site of Disabled Sports USA, at www.dsusa.org and see their chapter listings shown by state or you can telephone either 301-217-0960 or 301-217-9736   to request a general information packet.   This is an organization which was established in 1967 by disabled Vietnam veterans for those with war injuries but now has developed into a nationwide offering of sports rehabilitation programs open to anyone with a permanent physical disability.

I was fortunate to have attended a two day clinic on snowboard instruction for the disabled led by Beth Fox who is the Education and Outreach Supervisor for NSCD, the National Sports Center for the Disabled (a member chapter of DSUSA), in Winter Park, Colorado. She suggests going to the NSCD web site at www.nscd.org, telephoning 970-726-1540, or contacting her via the Winter Park Resort site at www.skiwinterpark.com.   Their goal is to hope to "make sure that individuals with special needs can obtain the information necessary to have a terrific vacation or day trip no matter if they are winter or warm weather sports enthusiasts involved in individual,   team sports, or family activities."   Beth emphatically states that the organization's services offer "everything from referrals to accessible lodging, accessible transportation, lessons in Nordic and alpine skiing, snowboarding, snowshoeing, competitive skiing, family lessons, winter sports camps, and more."

Those of us who have been active members of the skiing and snowboarding professional organizations PSIA and AASI can receive clinic training for instructing the disabled in the category which we refer to as "adaptive" techniques. We are thus able to share in the satisfaction of offering to persons

174

with disabilities the physically and emotionally liberating experience of snowboarding.

It was due to such circumstances that I had the opportunity to coordinate with Beth while I was doing my own coaching of a disabled snowboarder. I used a questionnaire designed by Gwen Allard, Chairperson of the PSIA-AASI Adaptive Committee, based at Ski Windham, N.Y. I thereby sent information regarding my techniques for instructing Anna, a young woman who had had both of her hips and both knees replaced. Anna's spunky determination to succeed quickly led to positive results, and her learning experience became part of a Research and Development Case Map which was filed into a data bank for future publications regarding adaptive snowboarding. My coaching situation with Anna was written up as a profile by Beth and was subsequently published in the Winter 2002 issue of *the pro rider*, the official publication of the American Association of Snowboard Instructors.

Beth has recently contacted me regarding an article in the Winter 2003 issue of *the pro rider* written by one of her staff members, Tony Peters, about a blind woman whom he taught to ride. Beth correctly states that "there are many women and girls with physical, cognitive, and psychological challenges who have also learned about the freedom that snowboarding allows. "

This idea of adaptive snowboarding is not limited to an activity for the super brave or for those who are powerful athletes. It is simply an honest effort on the part of snowboard professionals to be open and inclusive in offering a chance for all to escape their everyday world and enter another dimension of life invigorated by the excitement of snowboarding.

175

13
Kitchen Duty and Resort Meals

It's sort of inescapable. Here you are, Betty Shred, away on vacation and still you are expected to do the cooking, at least for one night. Bad enough that you will be doing kitchen duty, you probably have a large crowd to feed as you are staying with a group sharing a condo. For many years we accompanied the huge staff from a retail store, the Ski Barn, on their annual employee trip. We would travel out West to a ski area where the staff would test the next season's products. As a large group, we would share condominiums and, naturally, have shared dinners. My specialty was always a major hit, so much so that the group requested a repeat each year, to the point where I came prepared by packing the ingredients:

Spaghetti with White Clam Sauce (serves 6)

3 cans minced (or chopped) clams
4 cloves garlic- minced
1 cup olive oil; use ¾ cup first
¾ cup chopped fresh parsley (you can substitute a tablespoon
    of dehydrated)

Snowboarding for Women

First put up water to boil and cook pasta according to directions.

1. In medium saucepot, saute garlic in the ¾ cup of oil. Warning:it burns easily.

2. Add the rest of the oil. <u>Be careful now. Do not allow the oil to get too hot</u> because when you add the next ingredients it will then spatter all over!

3. Add clams and clam sauce.

4. Add parsley. Heat to boil.

5. Simmer only a few minutes. Serve over hot pasta. (spaghetti or linguine).

This recipe serves 6 people, so be sure to adjust the ingredients accordingly if for a larger group. Buying groceries at a ski resort means paying top price so it is wise to simply pack along for the trip those several cans of clams, dehydrated parsley and a baggie of fresh garlic. If traveling by car, you could even pack a grocery bag which could include olive oil and the pasta. Assign out the salad (and salad dressing) to a housemate, have another responsible for white wine and a fresh Italian bread...and ENJOY!

While you're at it, it wouldn't hurt to bring along a box of breakfast cereal. The savings might be substantial even if you wind up leaving the box for the next condo occupant. Most of the ski areas have a breakfast menu in their cafeterias, again, at top price. If on a serious budget, plan to have sandwiches made up locally and brown bag it at the mountain. Or make your own of the standard: peanut butter and jelly, a bonus in that it needs no refrigeration.

If you are not staying in a condo with kitchen facilities, the best way to choose where to have dinner would be to ask your snowboard instructor for suggestions. Go where the locals go. Since most ski area restaurants do not take reservations, you will have to decide if you want to take part in the Happy Hour scene (usually from 4:00 to 6:00) or instead eat an early dinner. If you go to Happy Hour, then you probably will have to eat a later dinner which results in a timing problem in that restaurants can have an hour or more waiting time after 7:00. Plan ahead, especially if you want to catch that first chair at the lift tomorrow morning.

14

Conclusion

A friend of mine recently purchased a local ski area, Cortina Mountain Resort in Hunter, N.Y., and, according to their Web site www.cortina-valley.com, envisions it as "The Snowboarding Capital of the World! (Skiers Allowed)." That's quite a reversal from the way things used to be. There once was a time not so long ago when snowboarders were the outcasts of the snowsport world. They were only permitted to ride on specifically restricted terrain or not allowed at all at certain resorts. Things have changed dramatically for a number of reasons. Now that it is an Olympic sport, we have become more acceptable, and there are only very few ski areas in the entire country which still do not welcome us. I tend to believe that a major factor in this was that of economics. Ski resorts who banned snowboarders watched potential customers drive past and head to the neighboring snowboarder friendly resort where skiing parents and their snowboarding youngsters could spend the day together. Thus, the fact that snowboarding began as a youth culture sport forced the industry to adjust if they wanted to market as a resort catering to the entire family.

Today the parents are also snowboarding. I have given numerous multi-generational lessons either to a grandparent, daughter, and grandchild or parents who enjoy sharing instruction with their kids. It's a chance to bridge the

Snowboarding for Women

generation gap and start upon a new activity together.

Snowsports at major resorts are becoming more and more inclusive. In Europe one always could see winter hikers and even horse and buggy carts on crossover ski trails, but now here in North America we see a greater variety of activities. There are both alpine and telemark skiers, snowboarders, snowbladers, and the latest group, snowskaters, all sharing the same trails. Occasionally a snowshoer may appear through the woods. Do they all get along? Well, some cranky skiers still complain that the snowboarders scrape all the snow off the trails. I usually walk away and seek conversation elsewhere when hearing this because the statement is outright absurd in its lack of logic. I do believe, however, that the reason skiers do not like snowboarders on their trails is because the rasping sound of the board is frightening to them. That would be the more honest complaint, and I empathize. We don't like the sound either.

Another problem was that historically, the majority of snowboarders were teenagers which meant that being rude tended to be part of the snowboarding attitude. Now, however, with the ever increasing ages of snowboarders, eventually the teenagers might have to be seeking skiing as their alternative counter-generational sport! Because so many snowboarders had never been skiers, they did not have any idea of mountain etiquette. Nobody, skiers and snowboarders alike, is happy with trails blocked by seated bodies or the fact that so many riders do not call ahead "on your left (or right)" as they overtake you. Fortunately, one now hears less and less of the negative. Perhaps it wasn't really a culture clash but a lack of educated trail citizenry.

Skiers certainly have a lot to appreciate in the advent of

snowboarding upon the scene. Snowboarding engineering brought them those shaped parabolic skis which make carving such a delight, the new softer boots, the parks with their assortment of fun jumps and challenges, and an opportunity for families to do their own thing but still spend the day together on the mountain trails.

The statistics for the year 2001-02 reveal that snowboarder/skier visits for the season were 54.4 million with snowboarding increasing 29.2% over the previous year. According to the NSAA (National Ski Areas Association), the rider profile is rapidly changing due to a tendency for traditional skiers crossing over to snowboarding along with entry of younger adults and children into the sport.

It was almost forty years ago that everything began, when Sherman Poppen joined together two skis to create the first Snurfer. Within several years the Snurfer had started an industry influencing others such as Dimitrije Milovich to patent his design which later became the Winterstick and Jake Burton Carpenter to develop his prototype for what would become Burton snowboards. By the late 70's there were ads for the Burton board, Winterstick, Sims and then Barfoot, followed in the early 1980's by Avalanche. Those were the pioneers, and they competed in the National Snowsurfing Championship held at Vermont's Suicide Six Ski Area in 1982. It's been a long and exciting trip since then to the recent sweep at the 2002 Olympics of gold, silver, and bronze medals for the men's halfpipe and a gold medal in the women's halfpipe, all to the home of the snowboard, the U.S.A.

Today there are so many snowboard companies that a listing here would be impractical. There are numerous snowboard magazines which report on superstars of the sport.

Snowboarding for Women

There are snowboard camps for adults separate from those for kids, special programs for women, training courses for becoming an instructor, and rallies of all kinds. There are traditional competitive events such as the slalom and super G races, but there is also the boardercross and big air halfpipe contests. Being an Olympic sport has brought it into still another league and level of public awareness, yet after almost forty years, people are always thinking that it's only been around for a short time.

The bottom line is that you should know the reason Sherman Poppen experimented with a new way to ride down the mountain. He had wanted to create an alternative type of sled design for his **Daughter!** So, when people express surprise at your interest in snowboarding, just be sure to tell them that it all began with a female.

We owe it all to young Wendy Poppen, the original Betty Shred!

Chickie R.

Index

Personal Notes

These pages are for you to keep track of your own snowboarding history. Write down the date, resort, instructor's name, and what you have learned. You will be amazed at the record of your progress! It's also a handy place to write in the names and addresses of the wonderful people you have met.

Personal Notes

Order Copies
of
Snowboarding for Women
a guide for the Betty Shred wannabe

Yes! Send me ___ copies for $19.95 each plus $4.95 shipping and handling for the first copy.

_____ books @ $19.95 = _____
6% Sales Tax (VT shipments only) _____
add shipping and handling <u>4.95</u>
add $1.95 handling for each _____
additional book   **Total: $**

make check payable to:
Show Dog Snowboard Press, LLC
Box 1069
Killington, VT 05751

☐ ***Yes!*** I am interested in having Chickie Rosenberg speak at my company or organization. Please send me information.

☐ ***Yes!*** I am interested in taking a snowboard lesson at Killington with Chickie Rosenberg.

to arrange, contact via
www.SnowboardingForWomen.com